2021 Cherokee Nation riders Ronnie Duncan, Kaylee Smith, Whitney Roach, Melanie Taylor Giang, Shace Duncan, and Tracie Asbill stand in front of the Remember the Removal trailer that hauls their bicycles and equipment needed for the trip. The trailer features the various forced removal routes from the Cherokee homelands to the new lands assigned in Indian Territory (now within the state of Oklahoma).

RIDING THE TRAIL

Cherokees Remember the Removal

Traci Sorell and Will Chavez

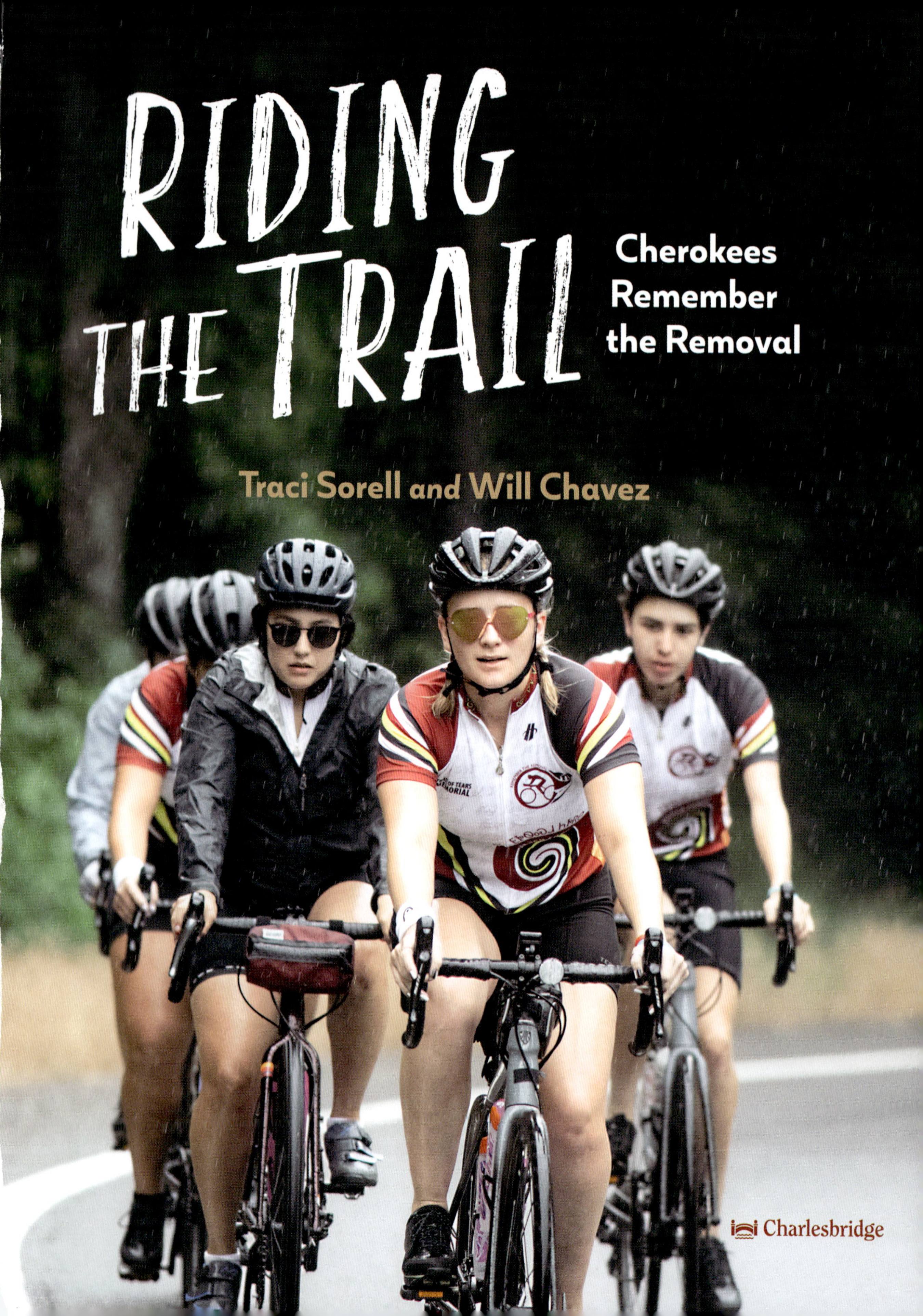

Charlesbridge

Cherokee Trail of Tears Routes
INDIANA
OHIO
KENTUCKY
NEVER FORGET
#RememberTheRemoval
Founded 1984
CHEROKEE NATION®

For Cherokee young people who are our future, and for our ancestors who survived the forced removal from our homelands.—T. S.

For my Remember the Removal teammates who have bravely taken on the challenge to honor and remember their Cherokee ancestors. And for my Cherokee grandparents, William and Cynthia Pettit, and all my determined Cherokee ancestors who came before me and made it possible for me to be here.—W. C.

Published by Charlesbridge • 9 Galen Street, Watertown, MA 02472 • www.charlesbridge.com

Library of Congress Cataloging-in-Publication Data
Available Upon Request

Printed in China • OPIC
(hc) 10 9 8 7 6 5 4 3 2 1
The authorized representative in the EU for product safety and compliance is eucomply OÜ, Pärnu mnt 139b-14, 11317 Tallinn, Estonia, hello@eucompliancepartner.com, +33757690241

Text type set in Blauth by Sofia Mohr
Edited by Karen Boss
Designed by Diane M. Earley
Production supervision by Jennifer Most Delaney

TABLE OF CONTENTS

"Let us . . . then inquire why the dear Cherokees are doomed to such miseries; have they murdered their white friends? Have they robbed or plundered? Or have they done any wrong to the United States for which that powerful nation is thus putting them to the torture? They have done no wrong to merit any part of this evil, their enemies themselves being judges, but by refusing to acknowledge the justice of that treaty made by a few individuals, in direct opposition to the whole national council and the voice of the people."

—Journal entry (July 26, 1838) of Reverend Daniel S. Butrick, a Christian missionary, who, along with his wife, Elizabeth, lived in the Cherokee Nation and traveled with the Taylor detachment during the forced removal

INTRODUCTION

They've waited two years for this moment. Today they leave for one of the most difficult journeys of their lives.

Bags packed. Bicycles loaded. Now they'll ride just under 1,000 miles in three weeks as part of the Cherokee Nation's Remember the Removal (RTR) ride.

The COVID-19 pandemic canceled the 2020 ride. The Cherokee Nation took the outbreak seriously and stopped all in-person community gatherings. That included the riders' weekly physical training and Cherokee language and history classes. So these riders continued training by themselves and also met online for language and history lessons. But now the availability of vaccines, which everyone participating must receive, gives them the green light to go. Still, caution governs the send-off ceremony on May 26, 2021, in the Cherokee Nation capital of Tahlequah, Oklahoma. Only a few family

2021 riders present RTR posters to Deputy Chief Bryan Warner (left) and Principal Chief Chuck Hoskin Jr. during a send-off ceremony in May 2021.

members, select news media, and tribal officials and staff attend. Safety is top priority.

Six Cherokee Nation citizens sit together—masked, quiet, hopeful, and a little nervous. They listen as past riders and tribal officers offer advice, encouragement, and prayers in the tribe's veterans center. The team feels the importance of continuing what other Cherokee Nation teams have done on twelve previous rides. The riders will honor their ancestors by seeing the places where Cherokee people lived and also where they suffered during the forced removal in 1838 and 1839.

That's when the United States government rounded up Cherokee children, adults, and elders from their homelands in parts of present-day North Carolina, Tennessee, Alabama, and Georgia. Soldiers—some from the US Army but most from state militias—used bayonets, or guns with a blade on the muzzle's end, that could be used to stab

2021 riders at their Cherokee Nation send-off ceremony in May 2021.

someone. Cherokee people had no time to pack anything and only grabbed a change of clothing or some food if they were lucky. Unless a Cherokee person had a horse to ride, they were forced to walk.

Soldiers forced children who were not on horseback or carried on their parents' backs to ride in a wagon. If the children or their parents showed any reluctance, the soldiers threw the young ones in and rode very fast over the rough roads. Some children received severe injuries from these dangerous trips. Once the Cherokee people arrived at the newly constructed internment (prison) camps across the Cherokee Nation, they could not leave—even though some were not far from their own homes.

From those camps, the US government planned to make Cherokee people travel nearly 800 miles to a newly created reservation (a smaller land base created for only Cherokee people) within Indian Territory—today known as Oklahoma. The US Army divided people into detachments (a military term for groups). Soldiers removed three detachments of Cherokee people from their homelands between the spring and summer of 1838. Many people died under the military's supervision.

Because so many died, Cherokee Chief John Ross knew his people would continue to receive inhumane treatment if white soldiers stayed in charge. Chief Ross wrote and requested to oversee the removal of those remaining in the camps. US Army General Winfield Scott granted him permission.

Chief Ross then called upon fellow Cherokee men—leaders in the Cherokee Nation government; those with wealth; and loyal men such as Hair Conrad, John Benge, Peter Hildebrand, and Richard Taylor—to organize people into detachments and lead them west. Some of the leaders had enslaved Africans, who were forced to accompany their

Cherokee enslavers. Most Cherokee people, including Chief Ross, and the enslaved Africans left the homelands between September and December 1838. The last detachment arrived in Indian Territory in March 1839.

Sickness, death, and harsh cold weather served as constant travel companions. Every day that fall and winter, the Cherokee people moved farther and farther away from the only places they'd ever known. Sacred places, familiar places—home.

Cherokee people refer to this time as ᏗᎨᎩᏱᎸᏍᏔᏅᎢ (dee-gay-gee-yee-luh-s-tah-nuh-i, "when they were driven [like cattle]"). Others have labeled it the Trail of Tears.

Now these six Remember the Removal riders will visit their people's homelands and the places where this horrendous chapter in their

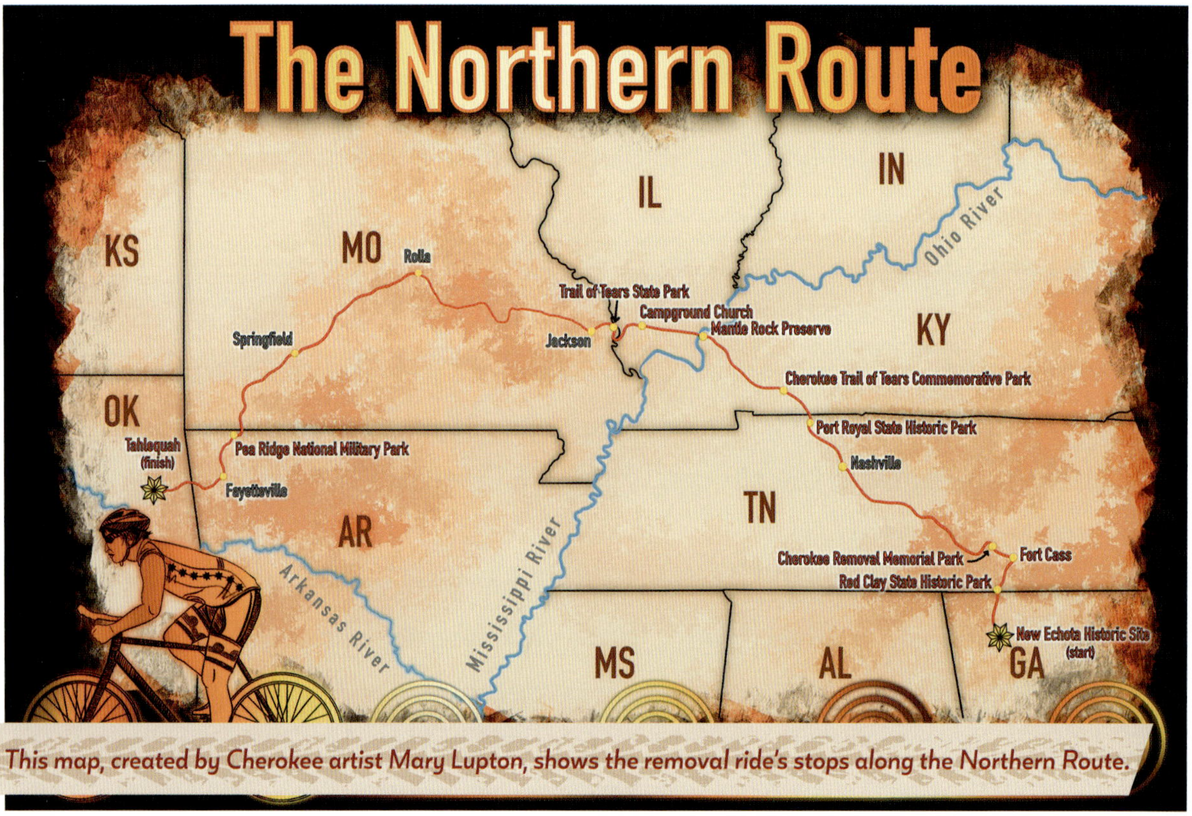

This map, created by Cherokee artist Mary Lupton, shows the removal ride's stops along the Northern Route.

ancestors' lives occurred. They'll be joined by three riders from the Eastern Band of Cherokee Indians, who live near the mountains of western North Carolina. Both teams' members descend from the Cherokee people who were affected by the forced removal. Their joint three-week trip along the Northern Route, the most-traveled during the forced removal, will connect these Cherokee riders to the history, places, and horrific experiences that occurred not even two hundred years ago.

With the send-off ceremony complete, the RTR riders pose for photos with loved ones and tribal officials. The team is soon-to-be high school senior Shace Duncan; college students Kaylee Smith, Whitney Roach, and Melanie "Mel" Taylor Giang; two mentor riders, athletic trainer Ronnie Duncan (Shace's uncle) and pediatric nurse Tracie Asbill; and a support team from the Cherokee Nation. After final hugs with family and friends, they load up to head east.

Riders receive a RTR T-shirt designed for their ride. Anyone can buy the shirts from the Cherokee Nation Gift Shop online or at the store to support the annual ride.

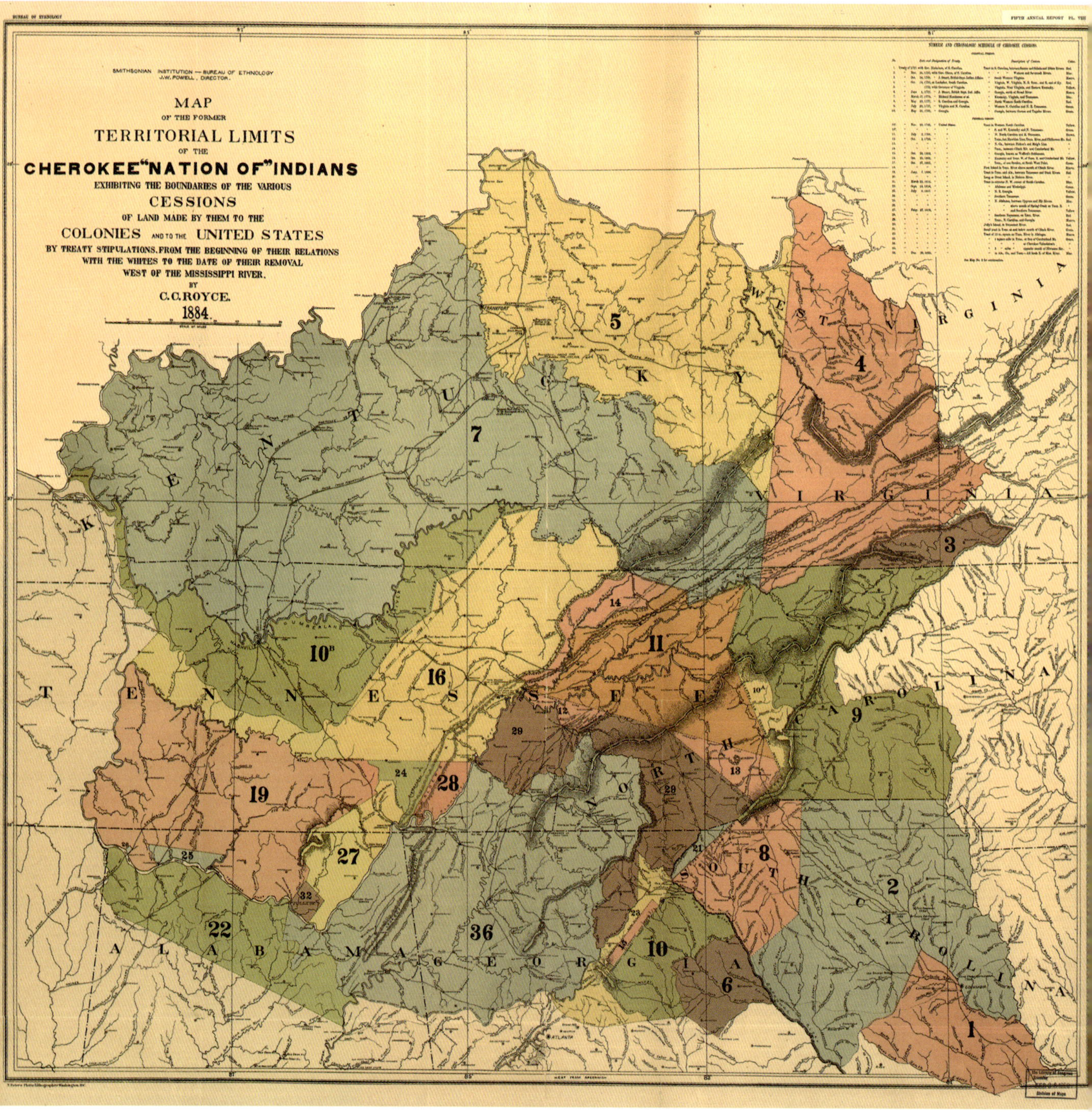

This map shows the large area of the Cherokee people's traditional lands, extending across parts of seven states.

ᎠᏯᏙᎸᎢ 1

ᎾᏍᎩᏃ ᎤᏃᎯ ᏓᏥᏂᏌᏙᏴ ᏗᏥᏂᏐᏎᏍᏔᏅᎢ

CHAPTER 1

The Path to Forced Removal

Before the Cherokee Nation sends RTR riders to retrace the forced removal route, they must teach them the history. Even though the forced removals of Cherokee people and many other Native Nations have been well documented, schools do not teach this information. The Cherokee Nation wants to make sure the RTR riders know how and why the forced removal occurred.

The Cherokee Nation's homelands covered a sizeable area in the southeastern part of what is now the United States. Before Europeans arrived, the Cherokee people operated as an alliance of towns in mountains and valleys across their large land base. A peace chief, war chief, and council governed each town. Each town council had representation from each of the seven Cherokee clans. The council had to come to consensus about an issue before action could be taken. Towns came together for celebrations, ceremonies, and to ward off intruders on their lands.

European countries did not operate like this at all! Their societies organized around concentrated power. Nobility (usually kings and queens and a small number of others with land and wealth) made the decisions. Christianity (the main religion of Europeans) centered men as the decision-makers.

Conflict occurred when people arrived in what's now called North America from various European countries, given how differently their societies operated from those of Native people. Growing numbers of colonies, warfare, the spread of diseases brought from Europe, and the capture and enslavement of Cherokee and other Native people made coexistence an ongoing challenge. The Cherokee people also faced continual clashes with white people when Europeans illegally encroached on their lands, even after Cherokees ceded (gave up) territory in treaties (legal agreements).

To counter these problems and the pressure to give up their lands, Cherokees agreed to draft a constitution in 1827. They adopted a central government with districts, and majority rule governed rather than consensus decision-making. This disrupted clan relationships and the balance of roles each person maintained in their family and town. Tribal leaders hoped their actions would show they meant to stay in their homelands and enforce their sovereignty (the power to make and enforce their own laws).

But both the colonies (which later became states surrounding the Cherokee Nation) and the US federal government continued efforts to minimize the tribe's sovereignty and shrink its land base. When a non-Cherokee person went onto Cherokee lands, the laws of the Cherokee Nation applied to them. Most white people didn't like this reality because they did not see Cherokee people as equals.

On top of pressures from governments, Christian missionaries from a variety of Protestant churches came to Cherokee lands.

They wanted Cherokee people to convert to Christianity. Some Cherokee children attended schools, operated by these churches, away from their families.

The changes to how Cherokee people governed themselves, the growing use of English in addition to their own language, and the conversion of many to Christianity caused disagreements among Cherokee families and communities. But that's not all.

Gold was discovered within the tribe's borders, which brought more trespassers claiming lands for themselves. Many wealthy Cherokees grew their fortunes by enslaving Africans to work their large farms. This spawned more jealousy among white people outside the Cherokee Nation who wanted more acres to do the same and enrich themselves. Calls for the tribe's removal in order to open up lands increased.

Splits occurred within the Cherokee Nation. Nearby Native Nations, such as the Muscogee (Creek) and Choctaw, had already been removed. After seeing this, a small group of Cherokee people known as the Treaty Party wanted to sign a treaty with the US government and go west. They started talking with US federal officials. But nearly all Cherokees wanted to remain in their homelands.

Some Treaty Party leaders signed the Treaty of New Echota with the United States. These men did not have permission from Principal Chief John Ross and the Cherokee National Council to represent more than 16,000 Cherokee Nation citizens. The treaty stated the Cherokee would give up seven million acres of land for five million dollars and agree to move to a reservation established farther west in Indian Territory. This new reservation was carved out of other Native Nations' lands, which caused the other tribes' removal to lands farther north or west.

When news about the small faction signing the treaty got out, the Cherokee National Council, including Principal Chief John Ross, called the document fraudulent. Over 15,000 Cherokee people

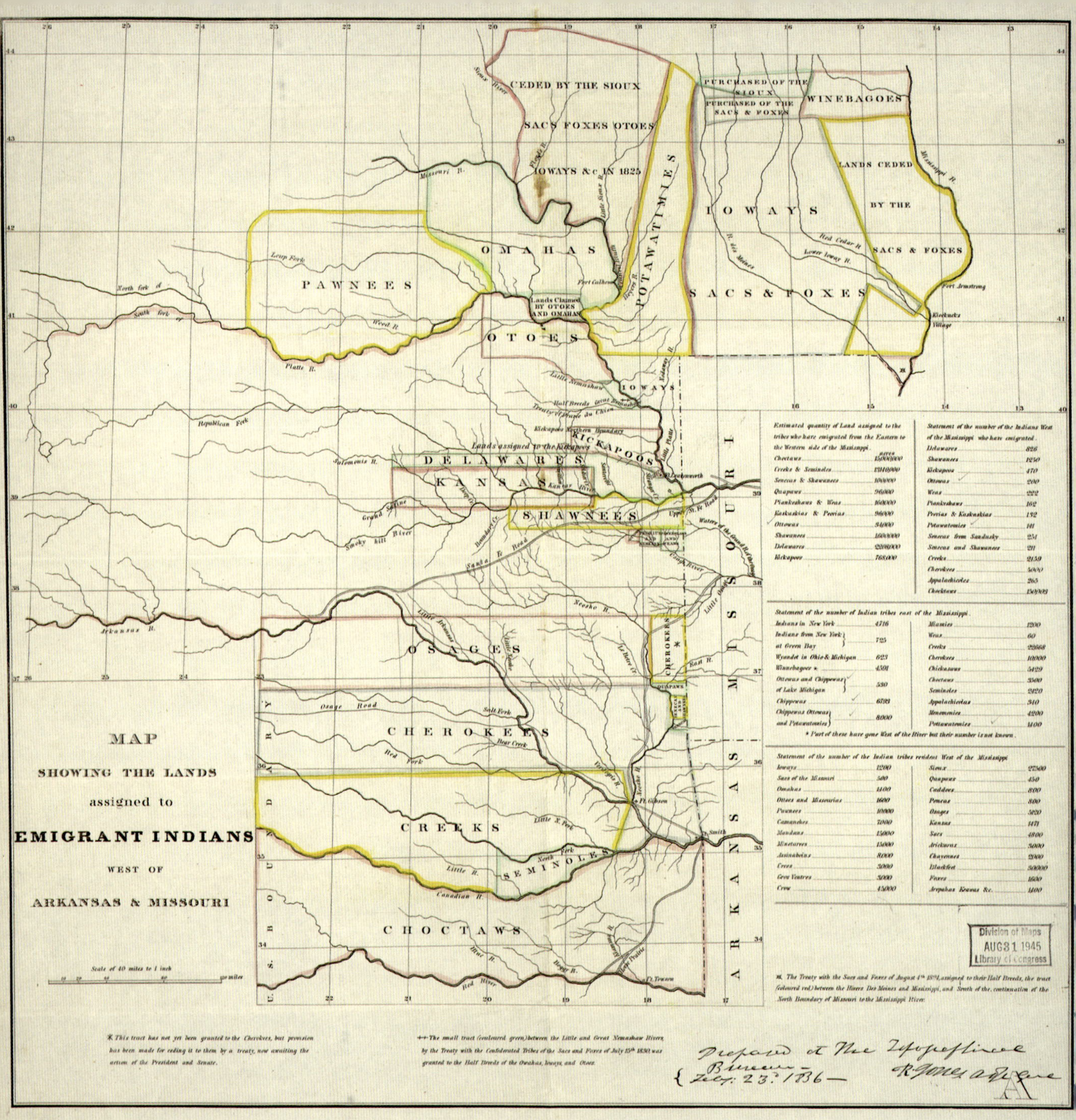

1836 map from Library of Congress showing Cherokee Nation lands in Indian Territory, straight across the top, and includes land above the Quapaws in what would become the southeast corner of the state of Kansas. The Cherokee Nation had to cede the lands in southeast Kansas as well as those in northwestern and north central parts of what is now Oklahoma in the 1866 Treaty with the United States following the country's civil war.

The reservation boundaries of the Cherokee, Muscogee (Creek), Choctaw, and Seminole Nations shown on this map change and shrink because of federal laws imposed on the tribes before Oklahoma statehood on November 16, 1907.

A FATEFUL MESSAGE

"I have no motive, my friends, to deceive you. I am sincerely desirous to promote your welfare. Listen to me, therefore, while I tell you that you cannot remain where you now are. Circumstances that cannot be controlled, and which are beyond the reach of human laws, render it impossible that you can flourish in the midst of a civilized community. You have but one remedy within your reach. And that is, to remove to the West."

—Message in a printed circular from US President Andrew Jackson to the Cherokee Nation, signed "Your friend, Andrew Jackson," written on March 16, 1835, just over nine months prior to federal officials signing the Treaty of New Echota with Cherokee men who did not represent the Cherokee National Council or Chief John Ross

signed a petition created by Chief Ross, and he delivered it to the US Congress in Washington, asking them not to ratify the removal treaty. But Congress authorized it anyway, setting in motion a disastrous removal experience for the Cherokee Nation.

To understand that experience, the RTR team studies what happened in more detail during preparations for their own journey. They read first-person accounts, such as the journal of Christian missionary Reverend Daniel Butrick, who lived among the Cherokee to promote his faith. He and his wife accompanied the Cherokee on the forced removal. His writing and other records include detailed descriptions of the hardships and death experienced during the journey. RTR riders sometimes find information about their own ancestors in these first-person accounts and other historical documents.

But how does the forced removal of 1838 and 1839 affect the riders and Cherokee people today? And what triggered the need for this remembrance ride in the first place?

The 1984 inaugural Remember the Removal team rides steel-framed bikes loaded with their gear.

ᎠᏍᏙᏎᎢ 2

ᎾᏍᎩᏃ ᏧᎾᎩᏎᎳᏅᎢ ᏂᏏᏣᏏᎴᏅᎩ ᎧᏃᎯᏏ

CHAPTER 2

The Ride's Origin Story

In the early 1980s, a growing number of Cherokee youth across the reservation were dropping out of school. They lacked the confidence and drive to see themselves as successful adults after high school graduation. This alarmed the staff in the Cherokee Nation's education department. Learning and developing one's gifts to share with others is a key Cherokee value. The staff got to work developing leadership initiatives to help young people build self-esteem.

The Remember the Removal (RTR) program was one of those initiatives. It centered on Cherokee youth riding bicycles and retracing the forced removal of their ancestors to understand and honor the powerful people they come from.

Dr. Michael Morris, head of the education department at that time, and his colleague Mose Killer knew that Cherokee people are strong, overcoming tremendous hardships throughout their past and present. They wanted to connect young people with their history and help them learn what their ancestors endured from 1838 through the late winter of 1839. The two men hoped the young riders' confidence and personal drive would grow during the trip.

One of the teens who applied for the 1984 inaugural bike ride was Taylor Alsenay. Encouraged by his parents to complete the ride application, the seventeen-year-old from Keys, Oklahoma, explained during his interview with Dr. Morris and Mr. Killer that he "wanted to know more about the Cherokee culture." Shortly afterward, Taylor received his acceptance letter and learned he would join fourteen

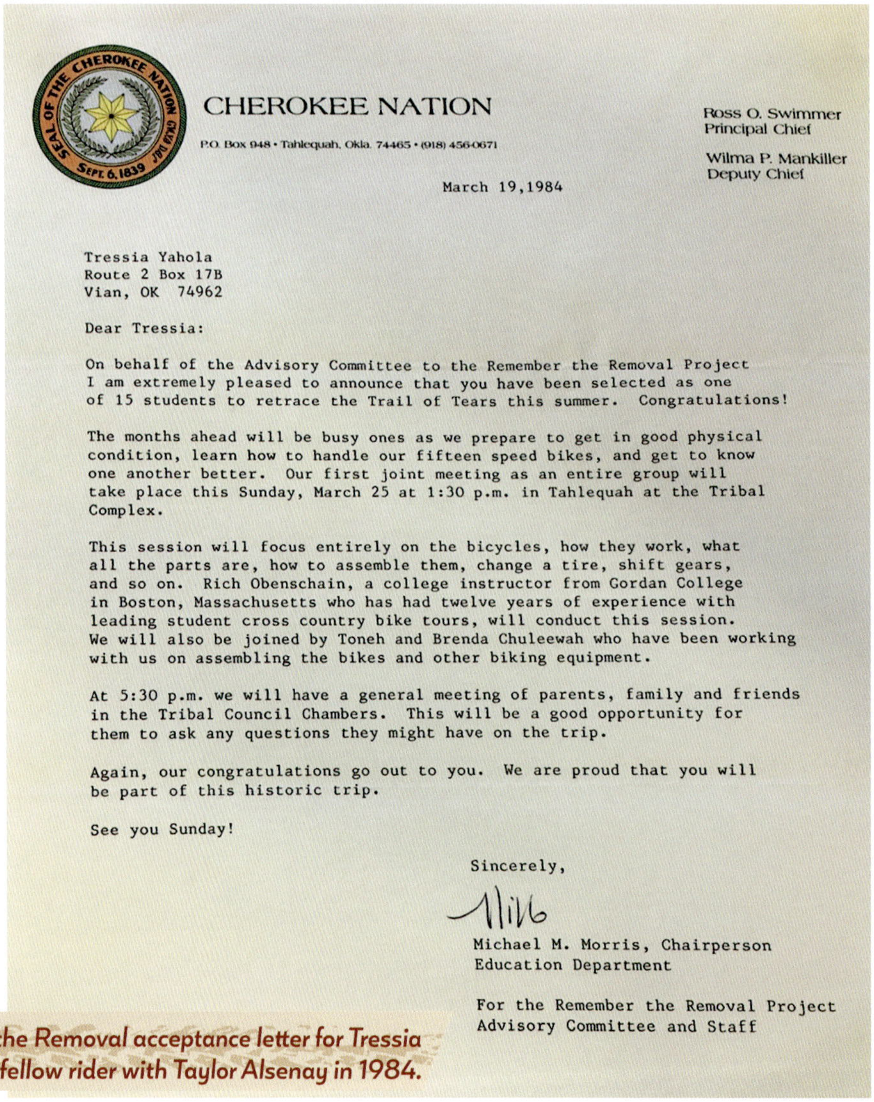

CHEROKEE NATION

P.O. Box 948 • Tahlequah, Okla. 74465 • (918) 456-0671

Ross O. Swimmer
Principal Chief

Wilma P. Mankiller
Deputy Chief

March 19,1984

Tressia Yahola
Route 2 Box 17B
Vian, OK 74962

Dear Tressia:

On behalf of the Advisory Committee to the Remember the Removal Project I am extremely pleased to announce that you have been selected as one of 15 students to retrace the Trail of Tears this summer. Congratulations!

The months ahead will be busy ones as we prepare to get in good physical condition, learn how to handle our fifteen speed bikes, and get to know one another better. Our first joint meeting as an entire group will take place this Sunday, March 25 at 1:30 p.m. in Tahlequah at the Tribal Complex.

This session will focus entirely on the bicycles, how they work, what all the parts are, how to assemble them, change a tire, shift gears, and so on. Rich Obenschain, a college instructor from Gordan College in Boston, Massachusetts who has had twelve years of experience with leading student cross country bike tours, will conduct this session. We will also be joined by Toneh and Brenda Chuleewah who have been working with us on assembling the bikes and other biking equipment.

At 5:30 p.m. we will have a general meeting of parents, family and friends in the Tribal Council Chambers. This will be a good opportunity for them to ask any questions they might have on the trip.

Again, our congratulations go out to you. We are proud that you will be part of this historic trip.

See you Sunday!

Sincerely,

Mike

Michael M. Morris, Chairperson
Education Department

For the Remember the Removal Project
Advisory Committee and Staff

Remember the Removal acceptance letter for Tressia "Tress" Yahola, a fellow rider with Taylor Alsenay in 1984.

other Cherokees on the bike ride. He said he "looked forward to . . . the adventure of this being my first time away from my home."

A week later Taylor and the other students and program staff met at the Cherokee Nation tribal headquarters in Tahlequah, Oklahoma. It turned out they would ride eighteen-speed bikes. Suddenly there was so much to learn! How to shift gears, ride in traffic, and ride as a team. The steel-framed bikes required a lot of energy and strength to pedal. Each weighed between twenty and twenty-five pounds. After adding panniers (bags to carry their things), some team members rode nearly forty-pound bicycles!

That first team fundraised to pay for everything they needed. The tribe didn't have the resources it has now. Today's riders receive support not only from the Cherokee Nation, but also from Cherokee businesses and a variety of nonprofit organizations. This allows the riders to focus on their physical training as well as language and history courses before they leave rather than having to expend energy raising funds.

But for that first year, the riders asked for donations. "There were a lot of noes, but we persisted and were sponsored by Quaker Oats and Gatorade," Taylor recalled. "We were so excited. As we trained, we started drinking Gatorade and thought we were kings!"

Besides fundraising, another stark difference between that first ride and the experience of more recent teams is prep time. The 1984 team gathered for their first training ride on April 14 and met only three times in May to train and ride together before departing by vehicle for North Carolina on May 29 to start the bike ride in early June. Today the Remember the Removal team starts preparing in December and trains for nearly six months to prepare for the ride through seven states. Big difference!

Original RTR logo first used in 1984.

The young cyclists on that first ride also made it their mission to remind the American public about the Trail of Tears. They talked to reporters from local TV stations and newspapers along the route about what had happened to Cherokee people in the early 1800s.

Because the Cherokee had been forcibly pushed out of their homelands nearly 150 years before the first ride, many people living in the old Cherokee homelands of Georgia, Alabama, North Carolina, and Tennessee had forgotten the history. Only the Cherokee-named mountains, rivers, and towns remained. When youth riders and mentors told people who they were and why they were riding bicycles through these states, some people said things like, "Oh, I thought the Cherokee were gone" or "I thought the Cherokee disappeared." Can you imagine hearing that people thought you, your relatives, and your Native Nation no longer existed?

The 1984 Remember the Removal ride covered approximately 1,200 miles and began in mountainous Cherokee, North Carolina (different from the current ride, which covers about 950 miles and

REMEMBERING 1984

Sixteen-year-old Marvin Cochran of Tahlequah, Oklahoma, couldn't help but remember his ancestors and feel their presence during the 1984 ride. While climbing an eleven-mile-long hill in Tennessee, he recalled thinking, "I'm on a bike. I could quit." But he knew his ancestors could not. Those who died were the only ones who left the trail. He said, "I know they carried me a few times."

Sixteen-year-old Marvin Cochran in 1984.

starts in New Echota, Georgia). That first team started biking in early June on what turned out to be the hottest day in about thirty years. A few cyclists suffered heat exhaustion and rode in support vehicles until they recovered. The rest continued riding into eastern Tennessee. When the team arrived northeast of Nashville five days later, disagreements about how to manage the ride began. Then the team's chaperones left and flew home!

As Taylor Alsenay recalled, "This is the first time I felt lost. We were stranded. Logical thinking and problem solving kicked in from the previous [Cherokee Nation–run youth leadership] camps."

The riders and support staff camped two nights at Twitty City—an amusement park next to country music artist Conway Twitty's home. Wilma Mankiller, the tribe's deputy chief (later its principal chief), came to visit the riders and staff in Hendersonville, Tennessee. Then they all went just a few miles up the road to the home of William Lee Golden, the baritone singer from the Oak Ridge Boys, a country music quartet. He hosted the group for dinner, and the riders camped on his lawn overnight before they pedaled north for Kentucky. What an unexpected and memorable outcome after being abandoned by their chaperones!

The riders regrouped with more supplies and encouragement after a new chaperone team arrived in Kentucky a couple of days later. Bill Glass, a former US Army paratrooper, and his wife Jean, a retired nurse, now chaperoned the team as they headed toward western Kentucky. From there, they crossed the Ohio River, rode across southern Illinois, and then crossed the Mississippi River into Missouri.

Unlike today's riders, who mostly stay in hotels along the Northern Route, that first team camped nearly every night. And remember they carried some of their gear on their bikes! Gear for today's teams travels in support vehicles, so riders carry only two water bottles on their twelve-pound bicycles. Also, no tribal law enforcement accompanied the first team—for protection and to manage traffic at busy intersections—like they do today.

When the inaugural 1984 team reached Missouri, they left what was called the Northern Route, used by a majority of Cherokee people to reach Indian Territory in 1839. The riders turned south toward Arkansas, where they followed the Benge Route, used by Cherokees in John Benge's detachment to reach Indian Territory.

That first team made it to Fayetteville, Arkansas, and then turned southwest toward Oklahoma. Once they pedaled across the state line,

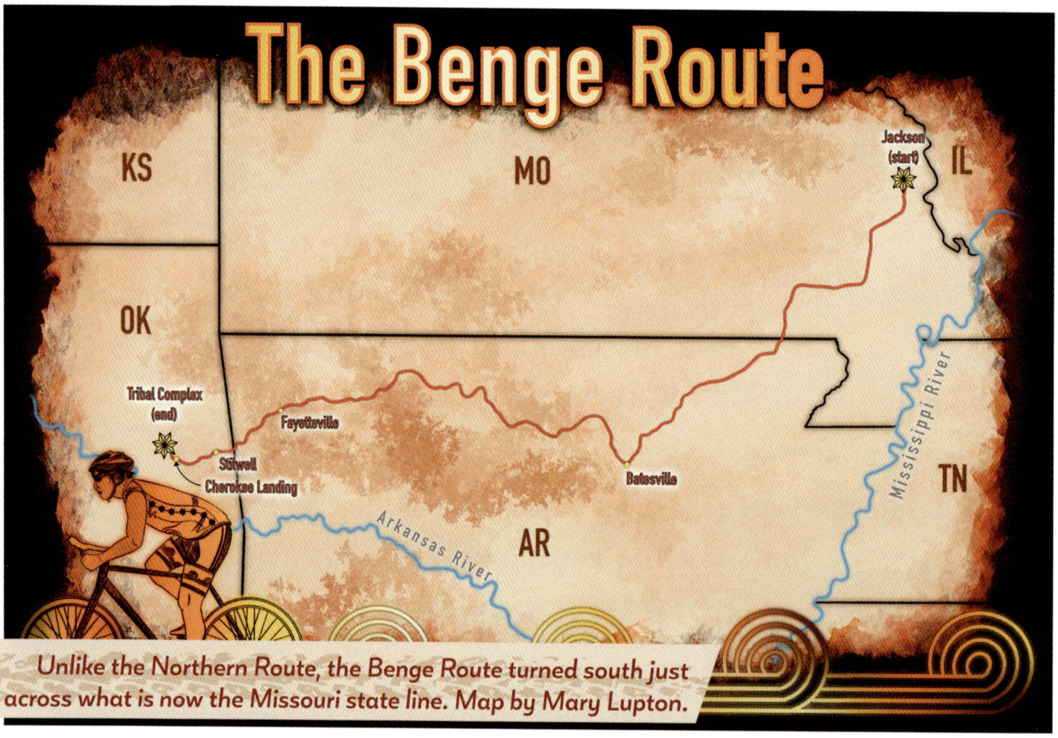

Unlike the Northern Route, the Benge Route turned south just across what is now the Missouri state line. Map by Mary Lupton.

the group stopped. Rider Jeff Robertson kissed the ground, and the team gathered for one more group photo by the state welcome sign. Traveling for nearly a month had made everyone exhausted and homesick.

Just a little farther west, Cherokee people (including some riders' families), tribal officials, and other dignitaries greeted the riders in the small town of Stilwell. The Trail of Tears officially ended here for more than 3,500 Cherokee people. After a brief stop, the team continued riding west to where a larger welcome party gathered at Cherokee Landing State Park on the north shores of Lake Tenkiller.

"Bear in mind by the time we were home, we were in outstanding shape and could fly on our bikes," Taylor Alsenay explained. "As we turned into Cherokee Landing, we were all together, and when we saw the banner across the road, the sprint to the finish started. As we broke through, there were many reporters standing in the road to get pictures of us! Traveling at top speeds and having to dodge reporters was quite an ordeal. I think their eyes bugged out as big as ours! Having avoided a near calamity, we stopped our bikes, and that is when you could hear the cheers of family and friends calling to the riders. There were many tears shed in excitement and joy for our safe return. We stayed our last night together as the 1984 Remember the Removal riders in Cherokee Landing State Park."

The next morning, the team rode together to the Cherokee Nation's headquarters. Unlike today's riders, they didn't get to keep their bikes. Budgets remained tight at the tribe, and everyone anticipated that next year's riders would need them.

Although another ride was discussed for 1985, it didn't happen because of a change in staffing, as Dr. Morris left his position the following year. A lack of financial support also contributed. As it turned out, the next RTR ride didn't take place for twenty-five more years.

Ever since the annual ride resumed in 2009, RTR teams have received strong support. But the daily difficulty of facing the unknown—weather, road conditions, and the painful history at each visited site—remains similar. Each cyclist misses home and their loved ones. They also recognize that, unlike their ancestors, they volunteer to have this experience. That lies at the heart of the Cherokee Nation's present-day selection process and preparation activities.

What do riders need to learn before the ride? A lot!

MEET THE 2020–2021 REMEMBER THE REMOVAL RIDERS

The teams selected by the Cherokee Nation (CN) and the Eastern Band of Cherokee Indians (EBCI) saw their team shrink in size when the ongoing COVID-19 pandemic caused the 2020 ride to be canceled. Some members' schedules didn't allow them to continue training. CN monitored COVID-19 case rates before deciding in April 2021 to allow the ride.

Back in 2011, the chairman of EBCI's hospital asked the CN ride coordinator if some EBCI citizens could join their western relatives on the ride. The CN administration agreed, and the two Native Nations have had teams riding together ever since. EBCI operates its rider program through its Cherokee Choices public health program. EBCI's riders must be enrolled citizens over age fifteen to apply, and the team does not have mentor riders.

The United Keetoowah Band (UKB), also based in Tahlequah, Oklahoma, is one of three federally recognized Cherokee tribes with ancestors descended from the Cherokee people forced to cede their southeastern homelands. The UKB has not participated in the ride yet.

These are the members of the 2020–2021 team. All information was current in 2021.

CHEROKEE NATION

Shace Duncan

Shace is eighteen years old and just completed his junior year at Sequoyah High School in Tahlequah. He lives in Stilwell, Oklahoma, with his large family—he's in the middle of fourteen siblings! He is also a founding member and vice president of 7 Ravens, a nonprofit organization that advocates for environmental protection within the Cherokee Reservation.

Whitney Roach

Whitney grew up in the Lost City community and now resides in Tahlequah, Oklahoma. The twenty-two-year-old attends Northeastern State University, where she is studying for a bachelor's degree in cell and molecular biology with a minor in Cherokee cultural studies. Whitney is also a former Miss Cherokee. She served as an ambassador for the Cherokee Nation, sharing traditional cultural stories and demonstrating how crawdad gigs are made.

Kaylee Smith

Twenty-year-old Kaylee was born and raised in Tahlequah, Oklahoma. She is attending Northeastern State University, majoring in American Indian studies, and hopes to be a historian for the Cherokee Nation.

Melanie "Mel" Taylor Giang

From Owasso, Oklahoma, Mel is twenty-two years old and lives with her family in Claremore. She graduated from Tulsa Community College with a marketing degree and will continue her marketing studies at Northeastern State University in Tahlequah after the ride.

Tracie Asbill, Mentor Rider

Tracie grew up in the Briggs community and currently lives in the Gideon community with her family. This thirty-nine-year-old mentor rider is also a pediatric nurse practitioner at the Cherokee Nation Outpatient Health Center and a lieutenant commander for the United States Public Health Service.

Ronnie Duncan, Mentor Rider

Shace's uncle Ronnie is forty-eight years old and lives with his family in Stilwell, Oklahoma. He works as a fitness instructor at the Cherokee Nation's Markoma Gym and serves as a mentor rider.

Will Chavez, Coordinator and Team Trainer

Will Chavez has coordinated the ride and trained Remember the Removal cyclists since 2019. Before that, he helped with the 2018 ride. But his connection to the RTR ride goes back to the very beginning. He rode as a member of the first team in 1984, right after his junior year of high school. Then he served as the first RTR mentor rider in 2017. He is the only person to ride both the Northern and Benge Routes on a bicycle. He trained the 2020–2021 RTR team for over a year as they waited through the pandemic. In addition to his paid duties for the ride, he also works full-time as an assistant editor of the tribe's Cherokee Phoenix newspaper. He's busy!

Eastern Band of Cherokee Indians

John "Bear" Allison

Forty-year-old Bear grew up in the Wolftown community of Cherokee, North Carolina. He is a professional photographer, videographer, and owner of a video production company. Both his girlfriend and her mother are RTR alumni, which prompted him to start riding.

Raylen Bark

Raylen is eighteen and was raised in the Wolftown community in Cherokee, North Carolina. Following the ride, she will start her sophomore year at Dartmouth College in New Hampshire, majoring in Native American and Indigenous studies with a minor in linguistics. Raylen is a former Junior Miss Cherokee and Teen Miss Cherokee.

Drew Johnson

Drew grew up in Cherokee, North Carolina. The twenty-two-year-old studies mechanical engineering at Western Carolina University. Watching his older sister complete the ride in 2012 inspired him to apply.

Corlee Thomas-Hill, Coordinator and Trainer

Corlee has overseen the EBCI program since 2018 and prepared a team for the 2019 ride. With the cancellation of the 2020 ride, she, like Will Chavez, continued training and working with her tribe's riders to get them ready for 2021. Corlee rode as a member of EBCI's team in 2015.

The 2021 Cherokee Nation RTR team stops for a water break during a spring training session.

ᎠᏯᏙᎸᎢ 3

ᎦᎪᏃ ᏭᎩᎸᏔᏂ?

CHAPTER 3

Who's Gonna Ride?

What do you know about the Trail of Tears? What caused it?

All Cherokee youth must answer these and other questions during the interview process for the Remember the Removal ride. Their answers help determine who is selected to participate.

Sadly, nearly all the young people who are asked these questions have limited knowledge about what happened to their ancestors and what caused the Trail of Tears. The forced removal of Cherokee people from their southeastern homelands to Indian Territory in the late 1830s is barely touched on in United States classrooms, even in Oklahoma.

But the challenge goes beyond getting the young people knowledgeable about the Trail of Tears. In addition to history and language classes, riders must also be equipped with teamwork skills, emotional strength, and physical fitness to endure the arduous journey. They will need to endure three weeks of riding an average of 60 miles a day—often in rain, extreme heat, and over bumpy roads.

between bikes is necessary to avoid crashing into one another or squeezing someone off the edge of the roadway.

When the weather during training doesn't cooperate, the team moves inside and sweats together in the gym. They strengthen their bodies, especially their legs, with weights. They also use stationary spin bikes to get a sense of what it will take to ride for six to eight hours a day as well as up hills and mountains. The fitness level required for riding 60 or more miles on roads is much higher than what riders can gain in gym workouts.

By April, the team rides 30 to 40 miles a day on Saturdays and Sundays, sometimes up to 100 miles in a weekend. But that's not enough to pass the road test before the RTR ride. So they must continue increasing their stamina and mileage on their own. Their trainer encourages them to ride individually or with other team members during the week. Team members who don't do the extra training usually begin to fall behind when the group rides together on weekends. Riders may be asked to leave the program if they cannot keep up with their teammates.

2021 RTR riders work to complete the notorious "Bell Route" toward the end of their training. The 44-mile hilly route is one of the toughest ones RTR teams face during training.

TRAIN HARD!

Autumn Lawless of Porum, Oklahoma, trained hard for the challenges she faced during the 2018 ride. "Training was hard for a reason. We were all ready," she said. ". . . our riders . . . were more confident, they were better leaders, and I wanted to be a better [ride] leader. I know I can push myself . . . now. This ride has given me perseverance," Lawless said. "The ride isn't just what you see in videos. It's not just people cheering you on and clapping for you; it's the time you spend with your teammates on the road motivating each other to get up another hill or just checking on each other. It really is a family, and there's a lot of behind-the-scenes work that goes into this ride."

Autumn Lawless, 2018 rider.

In early May, every team member must pass a physical exam and an untimed 60-mile road test to receive their riding kits (uniforms) and be cleared to go on the 950-mile journey. Any rider who does not complete the road test successfully is given a chance to retake it. Ridden as a team, the test simulates the hilly routes the cyclists will experience in Missouri and Tennessee.

Time to celebrate! Every 2021 team member and mentor rider passes the test! It is a special moment for the Cherokee Nation cyclists because they each receive their kit: three pairs of riding shorts and three riding jerseys. Art on the kit tops includes reproductions of ancestors' signatures written in Cherokee. The signatures come from the 1836 petition signed by more than 15,000 Cherokee people protesting their removal from their homelands. Seven-pointed stars representing the tribe's seven clans adorn one side panel on the shirts. The colors include red, black, yellow, and white. These colors are found in mound artifacts in the historic Cherokee homelands.

The riding kits or uniforms worn by RTR cyclists signify that the Remember the Removal ride is a memorial ride to honor the Cherokee people forced to walk the Trail of Tears.

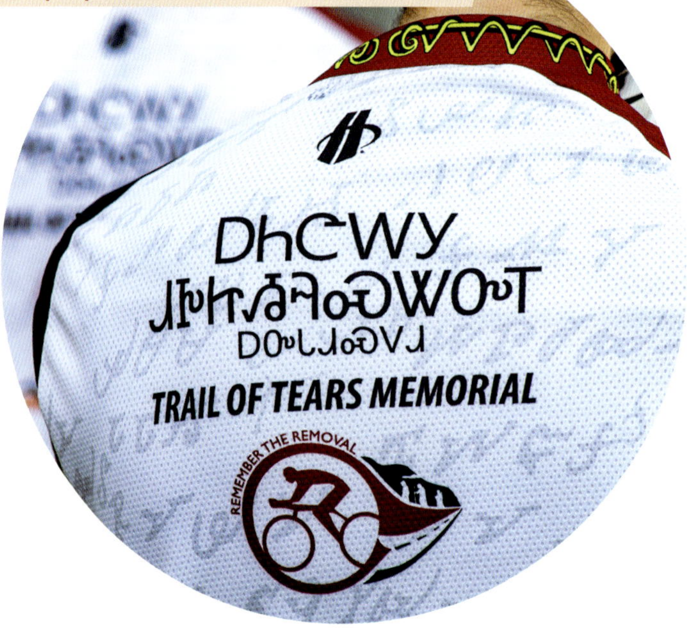

Along with classes and physical training, these riders must also be comfortable speaking with people they meet, from politicians to the general public. Support staff drill the riders with questions to help them practice responses to the media, whether a reporter in Georgia or a TV station in Missouri. Each rider serves as an ambassador for the Cherokee Nation and must feel comfortable talking about who they are, Cherokee history, and why they are riding so many miles on bicycles.

The 2021 team member most prepared for this requirement is Whitney Roach. She served as Miss Cherokee, a year-long ambassador role for the Cherokee Nation, and she spent significant time talking with the public and media at events across the United States.

2021 RTR cyclist Whitney Roach served as Miss Cherokee in 2018–2019.

The Cherokee Nation also expects riders to be mindful of how they interact with the public as they journey home. Rude people in public places or in vehicles who yell or honk at riders to get off the road are ignored or handled with as much kindness as possible. In those situations, the team takes comfort knowing a Cherokee Nation marshal accompanies them. When they ride, the marshal drives a patrol car behind them to direct traffic and intervene if necessary.

While the RTR ride accomplishes many things, its original focus to train and develop Cherokee youth to be leaders remains its core.

RTR alumna Hadyn Jackson of Stilwell completed the ride in 2011. She shared how it helped her become more independent and confident, especially with public speaking. "I'm usually not a people person, and I feel like I've come out of my little shell," she said.

On each day of the three-week ride, CN's team coordinator chooses a team member from CN or EBCI to lead the ride and another to ride as the caboose behind everyone. These two carry the responsibility for the ride that day. RTR alumnus Taylor Alsenay started this practice when he served as the ride coordinator in 2012 and 2013, and it continues today.

Everyone gets a turn leading. Some are naturals. Others find they want to do it only once. Experiencing this responsibility helps every rider understand what's necessary to keep the team safe on the road.

For example, the lead cyclist must shout information like ᎤᏲ (ew-YO, "bad road") and point to dangers and obstacles they see, such as ᎩᏟ (ghee-TLEE, "dog"). They must notice anything that could cause a cyclist to wreck or damage their bicycle. After the leader calls out, the rest of the riders use hand signals or verbally pass the leader's information down the line. The leader also sets the pace and pulls the group over in situations such as traffic building up behind them, a cyclist's tire going flat, or needing to replenish water supply.

Lead riders also speak to the group and pump everyone up when the team circles up their bikes each morning. The lead might relay how fast they want the day's pace to go or how they want to conduct the day's ride. Of course, weather, road conditions, and each team member's health influence the day's ride the most. Everyone listens to the leader's words before one of the other riders says a prayer, and they all do a war cry together.

Scan the QR code to hear the riders do a war cry before the day's ride begins.

Ride leaders also read short passages from the historical journals and first-person accounts the team studied during training. Doing this as the cyclists stop at various sites reminds them why they are retracing their ancestors' journey, that the Cherokee detachments traveled the same route, and what their people endured in 1838 and 1839.

Just as these riders' ancestors experienced major life disruption with removal, the lives of the 2021 team also underwent major disruption. They were selected in fall 2019 to ride in summer 2020. But the pandemic interrupted their plans. They witnessed many Cherokee families suffer losses, including the deaths of hundreds of elders who spoke Cherokee as their first language.

But now, armed with knowledge, training, prayers, and advice, these riders and their support staff must head east. It's time to meet up with the Eastern Band riders and start this long-awaited ride!

The RTR bike trailer is also used as a teaching tool, showing the forced removal routes and that Cherokee people still exist today.

ᎠᏯᏙᎸᎢ 4

ᎠᎴ ᎾᏍᎩᏊ ᎨᏒ ᎠᎾᏂᎩ ᎤᎾᎢ ᎠᏁᎯᏯ ᏧᏁᏅᏒᎢ!

CHAPTER 4

And They're Off to the Homelands!

Shace Duncan, Whitney Roach, Kaylee Smith, Mel Taylor Giang, and the two mentor riders—Tracie Asbill and Ronnie Duncan—pile into the large passenger van, along with Will Chavez and another CN support team member, who take turns driving. They're followed by more support staff in an SUV that pulls the RTR trailer full of bicycles and supplies. The Cherokee marshals drive their patrol SUV at the back. Excited chatter and short naps fill the riders' time between rest stops. The caravan of vehicles stops in Tennessee overnight before continuing east. Later the next day, they arrive in the Smoky Mountain town of Cherokee, North Carolina—EBCI's capital city.

The three Eastern Band riders—Bear Allison, Raylen Bark, and Drew Johnson—plus Ride Coordinator Corlee Thomas-Hill and support staff are ready to join the Cherokee Nation cyclists. The two teams have met virtually a few times, but in-person team-building exercises help the two groups get to know each other better. Jokes and teasing begin!

All the riders then go on a training ride to coordinate the road calls and signals they'll use. Rainy weather in Cherokee creates slick spots as the riders climb up and coast back down a small mountain. But everyone stays together, and the group appears ready to ride longer distances together.

The riders attend a second send-off celebration at Kituwah, the mother town of all Cherokee people, located just west of EBCI's capital. The tribe's principal chief, ride alumni, current riders' families, and community members gather to share prayers and good words for the upcoming journey. EBCI alumna rider Monica Wildcatt addresses the group and shares that when she decided to apply, she did not know how to ride a bicycle! She credits her family, community, and team with encouraging her to learn, train, and complete the ride.

2021 riders stand at the sacred Kituwah Mound site near Cherokee, North Carolina. The site is considered the "mother town" of all Cherokee people.

While at Kituwah, all riders participate in a blessing ceremony. Given the place's importance to Cherokee people, prayers said here are powerful. Reading accounts of Cherokee mothers, fathers, elders, and children forcibly removed from their homes was difficult in history class. And now, seeing the beautiful mountains, valleys, rivers, and streams of the Cherokee homelands in person brings those horrific passages to life. Cherokee Nation riders begin to feel the profound sense of loss shared by their ancestors in stories and historical accounts as they stand in places that the US government forced Cherokee people to leave.

To help riders understand where they are, the Cherokee Nation invites noted historian Jack Baker, a Cherokee Nation citizen, former council member, and the long-serving president of the National Trail of Tears Association, to join the group for the first few days of the ride. As the nearly 1,000-mile ride begins, he guides everyone and explains

2021 RTR riders gather with Cherokee historian Jack Baker for a photo at Rattlesnake Springs, an internment camp site where some Cherokee people were imprisoned prior to their forced removal west.

many important historic sites before and during removal across the Cherokee homelands in North Carolina, Georgia, and Tennessee. As they travel, he highlights that Cherokee people established towns along rivers and creeks for access to fresh water, food, and transportation. Mr. Baker sometimes points out where a certain rider's family lived, because he has studied each rider's genealogy charts.

One of the group's early stops is next to the Ocoee River in southeast Tennessee. There, cyclists visit the memorial to ᎾᏅᏰᎯ Nanyehi (NAAN-yeh-hee, known as Nancy Ward in English). Jack points out that this powerful Cherokee Beloved Woman and leader is an ancestor of Whitney, Shace, and Tracie. Nanyehi and other Cherokee women warned their children and grandchildren against ceding any more land in treaties with the United States.

Nanyehi's (Nancy Ward) grave near Benton, Tennessee.

Not far west from the memorial sits Hair Conrad's cabin along Candy's Creek. As a Cherokee leader, he represented the tribe in Washington, DC, helped draft the tribe's 1827 constitution, and led the first Cherokee-organized detachment in the fall of 1838. He is Tracie's ancestor.

With each stop, the riders feel a range of emotions. Sadness. Surprise. What has been lost and what has been uncovered about pre-removal life affects each person in their own way. As a group, they experience many emotions together.

The last stop on the pre-ride tour is New Echota State Park, just across the Tennessee border in northwest Georgia. It's evening now, just after the park closes. The park staff stays to allow the riders time to walk the grounds without the public around. Flags for the three Cherokee tribes—the Cherokee Nation, the Eastern Band of Cherokee Indians, and the United Keetoowah Band—hang just outside the visitor center. They are a visible reminder of how the forced removal divided up Cherokee people. Prior to the forced removal, New Echota served as the capital of the Cherokee Nation.

PICTURING IT THEN

It's not hard to imagine the capital buzzing with thousands of people when the Cherokee Council was in session. Riders tour replica buildings that make up the capital's main square, all located next to the Coosawattee River. Re-creations of the wooden two-story Council House and also the Supreme Court building provide a sense of the work that was done here. Around the square there are log cabins with one large room and outbuildings that show how the few hundred year-round residents—mostly wealthier Cherokee people—lived. The re-created home of missionary Samuel Worcester, who worked translating the Bible into Cherokee and operated the capital's post office, sits just east of the square.

On the south side, RTR riders climb a few steps up into the office of the *Cherokee Phoenix*, the tribe's newspaper, which is printed in both the Cherokee syllabary (developed by Sequoyah in the early 1800s) and English. The newspaper is still published today in the Cherokee Nation, in both print and online editions. Back then, the paper's readership stretched beyond the Cherokee Nation, and printed papers were sent to the United States and Europe.

The team watches a former printmaker and park volunteer demonstrate the intricate process of lining up type, tiny piece by tiny piece, just like *Cherokee Phoenix* staff did in the 1800s prior to removal. Once the type is placed, the printmaker uses a stamper to blot all the type with ink before turning a large hand crank. The crank moves the paper, which catches the ink before it rolls out as a finished news page.

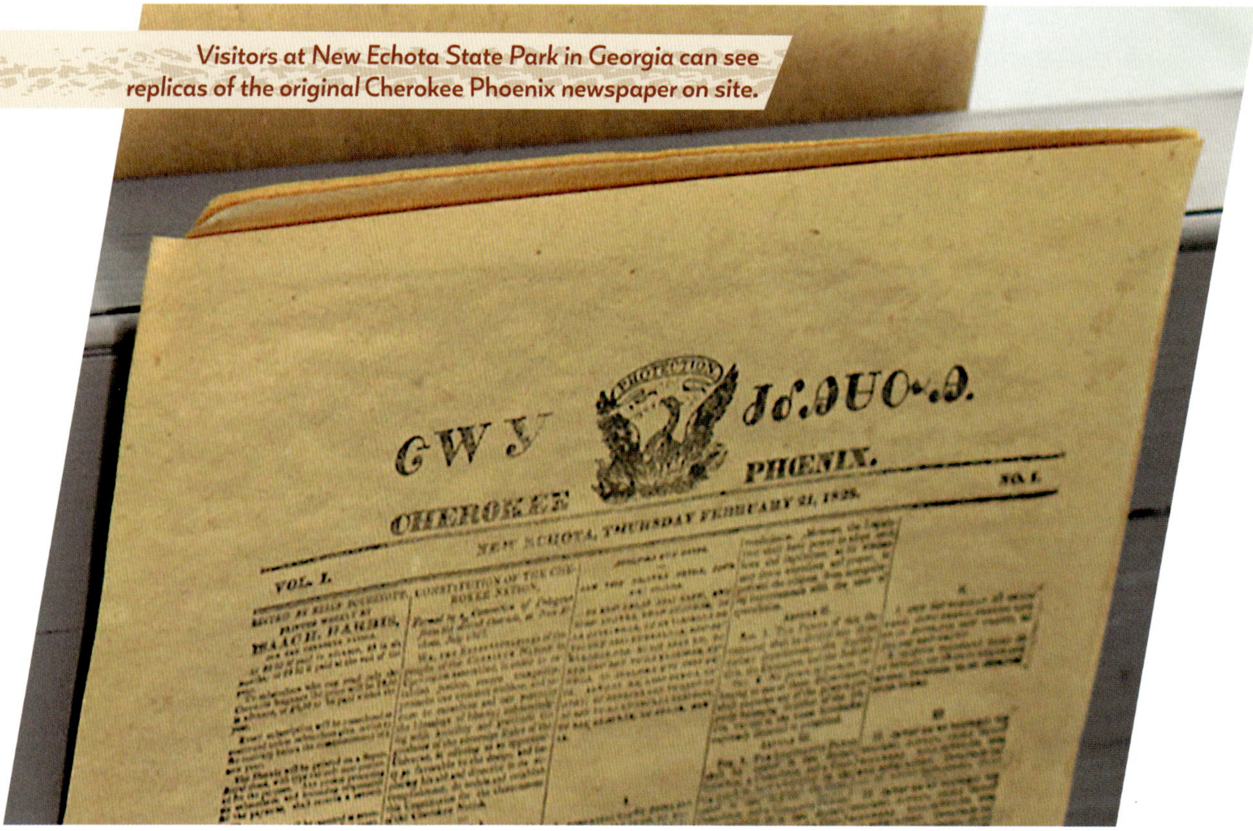

Visitors at New Echota State Park in Georgia can see replicas of the original Cherokee Phoenix newspaper on site.

Just south of the newspaper building sits a tavern. It functioned as a general store, hourly hotel, restaurant, and bar. People passing through the capital could rent a room upstairs to sleep for a few hours. A small window on the back side operated like a drive-through window. It allowed people on horseback to order food or drink and continue on their journey. The RTR riders learn that the window also served enslaved African people because they were not allowed inside. Just like the states around it, the Cherokee Nation permitted its citizens to enslave others.

The group stands and looks around. They're grappling with all they've seen and heard. They have a lot to think about. And they also have to return here early tomorrow to officially start the ride. It's a lot to take in all at once, and it's a preview of how the ride will feel. These riders have prepared. They are ready.

The next morning it feels like summer—even though it's still only late spring. Humidity saturates the air. But it's nothing like what the riders will experience as the sun and moisture combine later in the day.

Regardless, everyone's mood is light. Shace's dad and one of his brothers drove over 700 miles from the Cherokee Nation to see him one last time before the ride begins. Excitement fills the air.

Gathering near the New Echota visitor center, riders unload their road bikes from the trailers. Then they begin their pre-ride checklist. Each rider fills their two water bottles from jugs in the trailer and places them in the holders on their bike. Each rider double-checks their tire pressure and securely straps on their helmet. They slip on their special bike shoes with cleats on the bottom that clip into their pedals. The shoes allow them to ride more efficiently because their feet stay secure as they push down and pull up. So helpful when cycling 50 to 60 miles or more a day!

Will assigns Shace as the lead rider and Ronnie as the caboose rider for the first day. Each wears a walkie-talkie clipped to the neckline of their jersey, used to communicate with each other and with Will in the lead vehicle. Shace watches for and calls out hazards on the road ahead and gives directions to the group like the team has practiced for months. Ronnie cycles at the back of the pack, watching for any trouble with bikes, offering encouraging words, and keeping an eye out for hazards too.

The group circles up their bikes in the parking lot. Tracie says a prayer. Bear does a war cry, and the rest of the group answers. Jack Baker lets the group know he'll drive ahead and meet them at each site to share more history. Will then gives the team last-minute instructions before Shace leads them out of the park.

Send-off from New Echota State Park.

A dedicated team surrounds the riders to keep them safe on this long journey. The support-staff members drive the vehicles that pull the bike trailers for both tribes, and they leave first and stay miles ahead of the riders. Imagine how long the traveling caravan would be if they stayed with the group! The support staff sets up snack breaks, has sunscreen ready for riders, and prepares sandwiches for lunch at places that have restrooms available and space large enough for all the vehicles to park.

The riders always travel with the Cherokee Nation's passenger van in front and its marshal behind. Will, Corlee, and a CN support-staff person travel in the passenger van, keeping watch over the team in the rearview and side mirrors. Will and other CN support staff members take turns driving the vehicle each day.

The marshal is a Cherokee Nation law enforcement officer who scouts the road and surrounding area for any hazards. The marshal also watches to see if traffic backs up behind the group. If so, they signal the group to pull over where it's safe in order to let the vehicles pass. Cyclists pedal between 15 and 20 miles per hour. That's a lot slower than cars! The marshal also communicates with local law enforcement along the way. They provide tips about the best way to get around road construction or provide a police escort through a busy area when needed.

With everyone ready, now it's time to ride!

RTR members descend the hill, pedal fast to gain momentum, and then slingshot up the next one.

ᎠᏯᏙᎸᎢ 5

ᏗᏕᏣᏲᏅᎩ ᎾᏍᎩ ᏧᎾᏁᎵᏔᏅᏛ

CHAPTER 5

Rounding Up the Ancestors

Less than 20 miles north of New Echota, the RTR team stops at the Vann House, now a state historic site, in Chatsworth, Georgia. It stands as an example of how acculturation (adapting to a new culture) and assimilation (becoming part of a new group) did not help Cherokee people prior to removal. Owned by Cherokee Nation citizen James Vann and then his son Joseph following James's death, the 1,000-acre Diamond Hill plantation enslaved more than one hundred African people. The enslaved people picked cotton, grew corn, raised cattle, and took care of the Vann family and farm. James Vann was known for his cruelty toward those he enslaved.

When the RTR team arrives at the Vann House, the site's staff greets the riders with homemade smoothies to refresh them before a tour. The drinks are cold and yummy—unlike the thick, wet air pressing in from all sides. The cyclists walk through the two-and-a-half-story brick house that has a floating staircase and outdoor kitchen, and they see other buildings—most constructed by those who were enslaved.

Ride leaders Whitney Roach, left, and Shace Duncan congratulate each other as the 2021 RTR team rides through Georgia on the first day of the ride.

The Vanns were one of the wealthiest Cherokee families. White people in the area were jealous and angry because they wanted land and riches for themselves. This family's fortune allowed them to avoid the internment camps. But they still had to get out of Georgia. The state had passed numerous laws making it illegal for the Cherokee government to operate within its borders and for Cherokee people to do any business legally. So the Vann family traveled just north to Tennessee, and eventually they did move west to Indian Territory.

With the sun now high overhead at the historic site, the team climbs back on their bikes. They cross into Tennessee and head to the last temporary capital of the Cherokee Nation. After Georgia drove out the last two thousand Cherokees, refugees gathered in Red Clay, now a state park near Cleveland, Tennessee.

The team escapes the heat by watching a film in the park's air-conditioned visitor center. The film explains how Cherokee leaders

Shace Duncan acknowledges the camera as the team makes its way down the road in Tennessee.

and citizens gathered at Red Clay for eleven general councils between 1832 and 1837 to protest the removal and to work nonstop to try to keep it from happening.

After the movie, the group tours the grounds. They learn that there were ninety-one buildings on this land in 1836, from meeting houses to sleeping cabins. Today only a few replicas remain.

Then the riders climb a small incline. From there they can see the Eternal Flame memorial, dedicated to Cherokee people and those who died on the Trail of Tears.

Just down the hill from the memorial lies the Blue Hole. This fresh-water spring with a year-round temperature of 55–60 degrees produces more than 400,000 gallons of clear water each day.

ORIGINAL FIRE STILL TODAY

The eternal flame comes from the original council fire that the Cherokee kept burning when they lived at Red Clay just prior to the removal. Four Cherokee men took coals in iron pots and kept the fire going all the way to Indian Territory after people were forced out of Tennessee. It remained burning since after removal, maintained by Cherokee people who survived and rebuilt their nation. In 1984, the Cherokee Nation and Eastern Band of Cherokee Indians met in Red Clay to bring some of that original fire back in order to honor what their ancestors endured.

Cherokee people living at Red Clay used it as their water source. It is considered a sacred place, and only CN, EBCI, and UKB citizens are allowed to enter the spring. Red Clay park rangers allow the riders access through a locked gate. Ronnie offers a prayer in Cherokee as the cyclists stand in or dip into the refreshing water.

Later that evening, after loading their bikes into the trailers, showering, and eating dinner, the group piles into the passenger van. They follow Jack Baker to the site of the former Brainerd Mission, where Reverend Butrick was stationed prior to removal. In the cemetery, the riders take turns reading aloud from Butrick's journal about the burials there of Cherokees who died in the internment camps.

It's difficult to hear about all the abuses done to Cherokee people while they were driven from their homes to the camps. White soldiers sexually assaulted women and children, shot elders, and left others to die. Many Cherokee came to the mission seeking medical attention for mistreatment, illness, or disease. The riders shed tears, share hugs, put down blessed tobacco to honor the lives lost, and say prayers for all their ancestors before heading back to the hotel.

The next day—day two—the riders know what to expect. Someone will lead, someone will ride caboose, and again today will not be easy. They will start at Red Clay and visit an area covering 30 to 40 square miles where thousands of Cherokee children, adults, and elders found themselves rounded up to live in squalor until their forced removal west.

The reverend's journal entries detail each day's horrors and the filthy conditions in the internment camps where Cherokee people were forced to stay. These temporary holding camps interned, or kept, Cherokee people like prisoners. They tried to survive in cramped, unsanitary conditions often just miles from their own homes. The US Army did not provide enough food, fresh water, clothing, or adequate shelter.

Thousands of Cherokee people lived a nightmare inside internment camps set up by the US Army. Lack of clean water, sanitation, and medicine caused sicknesses like dysentery and cholera as well as death for many Cherokee. When the Cherokee leaders took over organizing the detachments, people spread out more and conditions improved. But still more than 1,500 people died during the roundup and internment before the forced removal march even began!

The RTR team pictures this reality when they stop at what was the site of an internment camp near Fort Foster, located on Rattlesnake Springs, a branch off Chatata Creek. The riders walk through tall grass on the now privately owned farm to listen to Jack Baker share stories about what happened here. He tells the group that between two and three thousand Cherokee people were interned on this site. They mostly slept outside. The US Army provided canvas tents for the Cherokee to take shelter from summer storms, but the material wasn't waterproof.

Jack shares that the very last council meetings of the Cherokee Nation occurred here before everyone left. The riders put down blessed tobacco, say prayers, and some tear up, feeling the suffering of their ancestors intensely in this place. As the riders survey the area, they feel the heat and humidity here on this late spring day.

From Rattlesnake Springs, the team rides just a few miles north to what was Fort Cass. Like at the previous stop, the fort is no longer there. Cherokee people knew it as Walker's Ferry, and today it is Charleston, Tennessee. This place has played an important role in Cherokee life. Located on the Hiwassee River, Walker's Ferry served as a hub of trade between Cherokee people and the British, and then later trade with Americans. Non-Cherokees entering the Nation here registered to receive a passport to permit them to travel through the tribe's lands. After the small group signed the Treaty of New Echota in 1835, the US Army built Fort Cass.

During the time of removal, the internment camps around Fort Cass housed about nine thousand Cherokees and three hundred enslaved African people in very unsanitary conditions. The Hiwassee River Heritage Center has information about this story and the history of the Cherokee people prior to removal for visitors to the area. The center also hosts the RTR riders for a visit and lunch each year.

Riders tour the center's exhibit space before being welcomed by staff and sharing a meal together. They also hear from Melissa Woody, vice president of the Cleveland-Bradley Chamber of Commerce, who's in charge of tourism for the county. She shares, "I'm a human, and I live here, and I care about what happened here." As riders listen to the center staff, they can tell these folks want to be good stewards of the Cherokee homelands and history.

Behind the center, riders stroll along the National Trail of Tears Tribute, a path and walkway that honor those who died during the removal. They read displays featuring "Voices from the Past," with Cherokee people and missionaries on one side and US military

2021 team at a National Park Service marker in Charleston, Tennessee.

and politicians on the other. The center hopes the tribute brings "the struggle of that time to a personal level" for visitors. The US National Park Service has certified the Hiwassee River Heritage Center and the tribute path as an official site on the Trail of Tears National Historic Trail.

The group says their goodbyes and rides west just over 21 miles to the Cherokee Removal Memorial Park near Blythe Ferry. What they've seen and heard this morning weighs heavily on their minds as they pedal away from another site of so much suffering.

Will yells Ꮒ (nee, "Look!") on the walkie-talkie, letting today's leader Raylen know there's unexpected road construction ahead. The asphalt road gives way to gravel for a few miles. Raylen passes the message back, and everyone looks ahead. Their road bikes have tires designed for concrete or asphalt, but not for small rocks and gravel. Slow down now, riders! The pace immediately drops. Will creeps along in the van so it doesn't kick up a dust cloud.

Once everyone arrives at the park, they visit the Cherokee Removal Memorial. A set of seven granite pillars representing the seven clans displays the names of Cherokee heads of household on the tribe's 1835 census. US President Andrew Jackson ordered this census to count all Cherokee people east of the Mississippi River. He wanted a list of all their property too. Why? The federal government wanted the Cherokee Nation and all its people gone, removed from their homelands forever!

That census came in handy quickly. The federal government used it to negotiate payment terms with the small group of Cherokee people who signed the Treaty of New Echota in December 1835.

Riders find their family's names, put paper over them, and color them with pencil to transfer the names. Seeing the names on the pillars is stark. Removal divided families. Some ancestors hid out in the mountains of what is now western North Carolina. Those who stayed or deserted the removal gave up their Cherokee Nation citizenship to become residents of that area. Some relatives went west to stay with the Cherokee Nation. Regardless of their choices, no Cherokee person or family—then or today—escapes harm or trauma from what happened during the forced removal.

The *Cherokee Phoenix* records video interviews with some of the riders about their experiences over the past couple of days. As Shace shares, "It's becoming real. This humanizes them [the ancestors]."

Melanie Taylor Giang makes an etching of one of her ancestor's names at the Cherokee Removal Memorial Park in Tennessee.

2021 RTR team members stand on a large map in Tennessee that shows the various routes used by Cherokee people to reach Indian Territory, now Oklahoma.

Escaping the afternoon heat, riders gulp water to cool off inside the meeting room of the visitor center, and they munch on a few snacks. Members of the Tennessee chapter of the Trail of Tears Association are there to welcome and host the group. Everyone listens to Jack Baker talk about this location before he tells them ᏙᏓᏓᎪᎲᎢ (doe-dah-dah-go-huh-EEE, "until I see you all again"). He will meet up with the group at the end of their journey in Tahlequah.

Now it's time to snap helmets in place and clip shoes into pedals again. Steamy, warm air still hangs over the area. Luckily for the riders, the road from the park down to Blythe Ferry is paved. They pedal to the water's edge where the Tennessee and Hiwassee Rivers come together. This confluence (junction) holds a powerful significance for the Cherokee.

Imagine that once you cross a body of water, never again will you see where you have lived all your life. That is exactly what happened to about nine thousand Cherokee children, adults, and elders ferried across this river confluence. Once they boarded the flatboats (vessels for crossing shallow water), almost none saw their homelands again. They entered the United States. Along their journey, they encountered US citizens who treated them as cruelly as the army soldiers and the white people who ran them out of their homelands.

They were cold, tired, brokenhearted, and forced to keep going until they reached the new reservation in Indian Territory—if they survived. They carried sacred fire, stories of the places they knew in the homelands, and each other.

For the riders, it's a quiet passage across the confluence. They divide into two groups because the boat is too small to fit everyone plus bikes. Each group wheels their bicycles onto the 20-by-10-foot pontoon boat driven by a local resident.

No one speaks on either trip. They look back at the homelands, then forward to the other side of the river. Each participant sits with the reality that this is a true departure. Absolutely nothing was the same for their ancestors after their arrival on the opposite shore.

As each group boards the pontoon, Will shares, "After this point, it's a grave tour from here."

2021 RTR riders pause for a photo on the edge of the Tennessee River after visiting the Cherokee Removal Memorial Park. Their ancestors crossed this river on flatboats as they made their way west on the Trail of Tears.

Riders load their bikes onto the pontoon boat for the solemn trip across the confluence.

ᎠᏍᏙᏙᎢ 6

ᎦᎰᏌᏙᏴ ᎤᏣᏗᎾ ᏂᏓᏩᏓᏧᏅ ᎾᏍᎩ ᏧᏁᏯᏅᎡ ᎦᎡᎯ

CHAPTER 6

Forced Away from the Homelands

The river crossing is a key part of the riders' journey. Crossing the confluence on the pontoon boat gives the riders a perspective on their ancestors' journey that they wouldn't have if they'd pedaled across the bridge. The state of Tennessee finally built a bridge for vehicles in 1994. Before that, everyone still used Blythe Ferry to cross.

Support staff drive across the bridge to meet the riders at the boat ramp on the other side. With the river crossing complete, the riders load their bicycles into the trailers. After a short drive, the group follows the usual routine. They check into a hotel, shower, and then eat dinner. Tonight they head to a laundromat to wash their riding kits. They sweat through each kit multiple times a day!

Tomorrow the Cumberland Plateau awaits—the highest elevation of the ride at 3,000 feet above sea level. It consists of two mountains with a valley in between. These mountains aren't high when you think about the Cascades or the Sierra Nevada on the west side of the continent. But it's still a good workout to ride a bicycle over both of them.

After a good night's rest, the riders circle up. Tracie offers a prayer. Ronnie's the lead rider, and Bear rides caboose. Today looks like a wet, slippery ride in the mountains. Forecasted rain shows up just as riders hit the base of the mountain.

Cherokee Nation mentor rider Ronnie Duncan leads the RTR team on their rainy ride up the first of two mountains near Dayton, Tennessee.

On the way up, Ronnie's back tire slips when he pedals to take off. Raylen is close behind and hits his tire. *BAM!* Down they both go.

Whew. Thankfully it's a minor collision. No major injuries, just some scrapes. Both bikes are in good shape.

As much as everyone wants to get over these two mountains, the goal remains to get everyone to the other side safely. The riders know from reading Butrick's journal entries that crossing the Cumberland Plateau was not only dangerous but deadly for many Cherokee people during the removal.

FROM REVEREND DANIEL S. BUTRICK'S JOURNAL

MONDAY, NOVEMBER 5, 1838

We started very early, with br. McPhaerson. His waggon leads the way for the whole detachment. We soon came to Walden's ridge, and ascended it, a steep mountain about one mile & half from the bottom to the top.

Ascending this hill, Little Broom's waggon broke, & he was obliged to stop & repair it.

Two or three other families also stopped, to return and bury an aged relative, who had been long sick. When passing that narrow & dangerous part of the road on the side hill, her waggon turned over & hurt her so that she died soon after, not being able to be moved but a few rods.

FRIDAY, NOVEMBER 9, 1838

We descended the mountain. The ground was frozen and the mountain steep, and the descent very long, so that I became alarmed, fearing I could scarcely get down with our carryall, though we had no load. It seemed to me almost impossible for heavy waggons to descend without damage, yet all came down safe, and we camped on Collin's river in Warren County, Tenn.

Everyone arrives safely at the top. There are screams of relief and joy, hugs, and tears of celebration. The morning's constant sprinkles turn into sporadic rain showers.

During a break in the rain, the team arrives at Fall Creek Falls State Park. Jumping into waterfalls, crossing a suspension bridge, and swimming feels refreshing after today's strenuous ride!

During the removal journey, Cherokee people slept in a tent if they had one. The original 1984 RTR team camped nearly their entire ride. Today's teams stay in hotels most nights. The 2021 team has their camping gear to stay at the park, but there'll be no camping tonight. Weather radars show strong thunderstorms headed straight for the park and nearby campgrounds.

The team must load up and drive an hour to find the nearest hotel before the storm hits. The riders give thanks again for their support teams who keep track of the weather and make arrangements to get them out of the area. Cherokee ancestors could not escape the cold fall and winter weather when they stayed here in late 1838 and early 1839. Several rounds of strong thunderstorms move through the area overnight and stay around into the next morning.

The continued stormy weather makes for a very late start on what is the team's second-longest day of riding—71 miles! Despite the rainy, and now chilly, weather, riders unload their bikes back at the state park in the morning to pick up the trail again. They head northwest at a good pace.

Along the route, the team stops at the Shellsford Baptist Church in McMinnville, Tennessee. There they visit an unmarked grave from the removal era with crude stones stacked and marked with the Cherokee syllabary in the cemetery next to the church. Whitney leads the group in singing the hymn "Amazing Grace" in Cherokee at the unmarked mass gravesite to honor the Cherokee buried there.

2021 riders sing "Amazing Grace" in Cherokee at a mass Cherokee grave near McMinnville, Tennessee.

Kaylee talks about the difficulty of visiting these unmarked graves and others during the ride, saying, "A couple of times . . . we would visit a cemetery of unknown Cherokee people. And there was one specific spot where they had stacked Cherokee people on top of each other. I think it was three or four, just right on top of each other. And it was an unmarked grave. There was just rocks around it. And then there was a smaller one with stacked children."

After lunch in the cemetery's gazebo, the group pedals on toward Nashville. But they must trailer up all the bikes before they reach Tennessee's capital city. Heavy traffic in the metro area won't allow the group to ride safely. Given the late start and long ride today, nobody complains as they climb into the passenger vans. Plus they learn that they have a dinner invitation!

Tracie Asbill's relatives, who live on the outskirts of Nashville, invite the entire group—riders, support staff, and the marshals—to enjoy a huge spread of delicious homemade food, including frybread. Tracie's

2021 RTR team members ride through the hot Tennessee countryside on their way to Nashville, Tennessee.

husband and three young children drive nine hours from Tahlequah to see her. Smiles light up everyone's faces as they share stories, jokes, and great food together. The riders end their night at a hotel northwest of Nashville.

The next day starts with clear skies. The team rides to Coopertown City Hall, located on the original Northern Route. The town's mayor, Becca Werner, and her parents, along with law enforcement and a

RTR Mentor Rider Tracie Asbill.

slew of community members, welcome the riders and support staff. Homemade breakfast burritos, chicken and biscuits, fruit, donuts, and cinnamon rolls fill tables in the parking lot. It is all prepared by generous volunteers. Two homemade meals in a row—what a treat!

After leaving Coopertown, riders pedal on the trail up to Port Royal State Park on the banks of the Red River. David Britton, the park manager, greets the group and leads a tour. He explains the history and role of this place, where enslaved men and women grew and dark fired tobacco, then sent it on flatboats to New Orleans for white landowners. But Cherokee people knew this area in their trading and hunting travels precontact (before Europeans arrived).

David always asks the group's permission before sharing any Cherokee history or stories. He's conscientious and understands his duty to do what's right. As a non-Cherokee, he knows these stories belong to Cherokee people. He's also very sensitive to the effect this visit can have on team members. The park's signage has information about what happened to Cherokee people and what leaders said

Port Royal State Park manager David Britton provides riders with a tour of a preserved area where their ancestors walked.

about the removal. It's jarring. David shares, "A violation of human rights is what happened with the removal."

On the north side of the Red River, part of the original trail has been preserved. Incredible! David walks the group down from the road to a field with some signs. Quotes from white politicians and descriptions of what happened to Cherokee people hit everyone hard. From there he leads the team to the river's edge and explains how the river would have been swollen with water in the wintertime when Cherokee people needed to cross it. Staying upright in a strong current of cold water seems impossible.

David and his staff then step back into the field to give the RTR team privacy as they walk onto the preserved portion of the removal trail. Bear gives each person a small amount of blessed tobacco to pray with and put down on the trail.

No one leaves the original trail at Port Royal unchanged. Like so many times on the ride so far, sadness, anger, and frustration rise up, only to be followed by joy, laughter, and connection with teammates and support staff. It's an emotional roller-coaster ride many times each day!

After Port Royal, the team heads north to Clarksville, Tennessee. Instead of a picnic lunch, they sit down for a meal at Olive Garden. This stop lightens everyone's mood before the group ventures to Dunbar Cave on the south side of town.

Guess who's there? David Britton! He oversees this state park too. He guides the team into the cave. As the group crosses the wet, slippery floor close to the entrance, David explains how Cherokee people knew this place. As the team walks farther into the cave, they notice a drier floor and less moisture. Yawns among the group increase because of less oxygen too! David points out petroglyphs, pictographs, and Cherokee syllabary on the walls. What a difference to see a glimpse of pre-removal life recorded here versus the suffering on the trail felt at Port Royal.

And what an emotional and adventurous day for the riders—one that will remain with them for a long time.

The next day as the riders circle up for today's trek, it's clear that the experiences yesterday at Port Royal have created a stronger bond among them. They hit the road for Kentucky, crossing what seems to be mostly flat farmlands. They visit Big Springs in Princeton, Kentucky, a Cherokee removal camp site along the trail.

Later that evening in Hopkinsville, they tour the Trail of Tears Commemorative Park. They visit two Cherokee graves belonging to Chief White Path and another leader, Fly Smith, who died there during the forced removal.

Folks from Hopkinsville host a barbecue dinner for the RTR team. Many who gather share how much better they feel having riders return this year. They missed the annual connection because of the pandemic.

Members of the 2021 Remember the Removal team walk on a preserved section of the removal trail at Port Royal State Park in Adams, Tennessee. After crossing the Red River, Cherokee people used the trail to make their way into Kentucky.

THE PORT ROYAL EXPERIENCE— IN THEIR OWN WORDS

Each of the younger riders shared powerful experiences from their time on the trail.

"Port Royal is one of the most intense spots. I went there kind of confident that I could keep my composure, but once you walk on the trail and [imagine] hearing the footsteps . . . it takes you to that mindset of being able to picture the ancestors being forced to walk through there. They were getting farther and farther away from their home."

—Melanie Taylor Giang, Cherokee Nation

"He [David Britton, the park manager] was talking about how whenever the winter comes, there's very high volume in this river, super raging. So I went down to the water and just looked at it. And it wasn't like water from home. It was very murky. The rocks look different, and whenever I looked up, I could just see this nasty cutout of this red clay bank. And I don't know, it just wasn't a peaceful sight. And that was one of the main turning points. And I felt . . . how the removal was also a very negatively powerful movement of just stripping a people from gorgeous ancestral land. It's like that water—it just rips from the banks. It just takes out those beautiful chunks of earth."

—Drew Johnson, Eastern Band of Cherokee Indians

"Whenever we were at Port Royal and we had entered the preserved trail where our ancestors' feet touched . . . you could feel all the negative energy as we stood there and we just spoke about it. But once we had walked down to the riverbed, I had crouched down to pray, and it just felt like something, or somebody, was hovering over me, and I began to cry. . . . That was just such a surreal moment for me because we have so much support on this ride.

We have water, we have hotels, we have clothes, we have food, we have people who host us, and just they give us so much. And our ancestors didn't have anything, and they were walking into the unknown. . . . But it was also empowering because if our ancestors hadn't walked into the unknown, none of us could be walking there today."

—Kaylee Smith, Cherokee Nation

"Walking into this part of the trail was a quick change of pace from the usual biking and laughing with my teammates. . . . I quickly realized why I was doing this. . . . Being able to conquer huge mountains, not only physically but mentally, is something that can only be accomplished on this bike ride."

—Shace Duncan, Cherokee Nation

"The park ranger, David, said, I'm going to let you guys stand here, and I'm going to let you have a moment, but this is what your ancestors would've seen. Walking along the trail, walking towards the unknown, walking into fear, walking in sadness . . . it was this very pretty place. But walking back after hearing . . . those words was just very heavy on the heart. I will never forget that day. . . . The atmosphere within the team definitely changed that day. . . . All of us collectively and individually realized why we're doing this."

—Whitney Roach, Cherokee Nation

"I'm not very emotional at all. And I cried once on this ride . . . at Port Royal when we got to walk on the actual trail. I got tobacco. I was going to put it down. I was just saying my prayers, and I thought I felt Bear's hand like a pat on the back or something. . . . So I kind of looked and there was no one there, so who could it have been? It was really emotional because I don't know who it was. I didn't know what to do. I didn't know what to feel, and just all of it hit me at once. And it was the kind of push I needed to finally break that emotional barrier that I had."

—Raylen Bark, Eastern Band of Cherokee Indians

While at the park, Mel shares how this has been an enlightening experience for her. But she is also very angry. It's difficult seeing the places she's read about, especially now that she better understands the emotional toll the removal took on her ancestors. Visiting the sites brings up complicated emotions. She adds that the Cherokees past and present are the same people. Indeed.

The next day, the riders follow the Northern Route and head toward the hills of western Kentucky. They see lots of deer, turtles, and wild turkeys along the newly repaved, twisty two-lane back road to Mantle Rock, located near the wide Ohio River.

Once there, the riders hike down through tall trees and across trickling streams. A large rock emerges in the forest tree line. Some wonder if Cherokee people sought shelter from the wintery weather

Mantle Rock is always a somber visit as RTR team members explore the site where Cherokee people took shelter for weeks during December 1838, waiting for the Ohio River to thaw to enable crossing into Illinois.

under this massive rock while they waited to cross the Ohio River. Ronnie says, "If I saw a big tree, I [was] always wondering if it was there when they came through like at the Mantle Rock place. I [was] looking at them trees like that one that went through the middle [of the rock]. I don't know if that was there or not when they passed through." If only the trees could share information with the riders about who passed through during the removal.

After the riders hike back out, they cycle to Berry's Ferry, where the ferry moved people and wagons across the Ohio River. Peter Hildebrand's detachment got stuck here in December 1838. Thick ice floes on the river made crossing dangerous. This forced the group to camp in the bitter cold. The same occurred for detachments crossing the icy Mississippi River farther along the trail. More people grew sick and died during the wait for the ice to melt.

RTR team members celebrate reaching the Kentucky state line as they leave Tennessee in June 2021.

2021 RTR teammates enjoy posing with a statue of Superman in Metropolis, Illinois, after riding through Kentucky.

ᎠᏬᏙᏄᎢ 7

ᎠᏍᏓᏯ ᏧᏒᎯᏛ ᎢᎬᏱᏗᏢ

CHAPTER 7

Hard Days Ahead

The cyclists trailer their bikes by the water's edge and ride in vans down several busy highways in western Kentucky along the Ohio River until they finally cross the water over the bridge. They spend the night in the small town of Metropolis, Illinois, known for celebrating the DC Comics character Superman. After dinner, the riders explore the town and snap photos with the superhero statue and other memorabilia.

The next morning, they head back to the trail. The caravan of vehicles heads northeast to the town of Golconda, on the Illinois side of the Ohio River. It's directly across from Berry's Ferry, and it's where Cherokee people landed after crossing the river. From there, the cyclists begin riding across the lower part of Illinois. Reverend Butrick recorded in his journal that white people in Illinois were not kind to the Cherokee people as several detachments made their way slowly through the wooded lands. Many Cherokee children became too weak and died. Local people focused on what money they could get from the Cherokee for supplying grave clothes and coffins. It's suspected that one Cherokee man was murdered by white people near Golconda after he became separated from his detachment. Then the murderers sought payment for burying him! The riders keep this history in their minds while riding 55 miles to cross the southern tip of Illinois in a single day.

What may be the toughest part of the ride now awaits them. Missouri—or "Misery," as the riders refer to the journey across the state—lies just across the Mississippi River. Crossing the state was not easy for their ancestors, either. They were weak, hungry, and sick from constant exposure to the cold from December through February. They buried many elders and children across the southern part of this state. Weeks of travel were filled with heartbreak rather than hope.

The RTR team spends just over a week in Missouri. They ride up and down hills on a patchwork of back roads that rattle their bicycles and bodies. The sun scorches them daily at this point in the ride.

Missouri's hills are unrelenting. The RTR team trains for six months to be able to climb those hills for 50 to 70 miles daily in June.

Before setting off on this challenging segment, the team gets their first full rest day in Cape Girardeau. But honestly, no one rests for the whole day. Laundry must be done. Vehicles need sprucing up. All the bikes have to be cleaned and tuned up too.

THE RIGHT THING TO DO

Since 2014, bike mechanic José Alcalá has met each RTR team in Illinois and followed them across the Mississippi River to Cape Girardeau. He cleans and maintains the bikes before the team begins riding west from Trail of Tears State Park, just north of Cape Girardeau. He shares, "I have been fortunate enough to put this on my schedule each year. It's just the right thing to do. My family, and especially my mom, taught us to share and taught us that if you have something that is helpful to people, you should do your best to try to help." Each team and both Cherokee Nations are grateful for José's continuing kindness and service.

Bicycle mechanic José Alcalá gives his time to clean and maintain RTR bikes when the team reaches the ride's halfway point in Cape Girardeau, Missouri.

Also while in Cape Girardeau, the Cherokee Nation support staff say goodbye before they head home. They need to return to their regular jobs. A new support staff team arrives from Tahlequah to help the riders finish their journey.

This transition often causes discomfort for the riders. They've grown close to those who have witnessed their journey and struggles from Georgia through Illinois. The team exchanges lots of hugs with the first group before they depart.

As much as the ride affects and changes the riders, it often changes the support staff too. They learn more about what their Cherokee ancestors endured during the forced removal. When the riders arrive back home, the first support-staff group will wait among the crowd of family and friends. They will cheer for the riders and the second support-staff group as they all arrive in Tahlequah.

With their new crew, the RTR team prepares to head west from Cape Girardeau to Farmington, Missouri. Kaylee leads on this leg—a 74-mile ride—the journey's longest day of riding.

Missouri is a grind. The team rides 50 or more miles each day in the unrelenting Ozark Hills and heat. Cherokee Nation's riders are better prepared for Missouri because their reservation usually experiences heat and humidity from early May through late October. The EBCI team trains at elevations around 2,000 feet above sea level and higher, and that means their weather is much cooler. It's only mid-June, and the summer solstice is over a week away. But the heat and humidity still sap everyone's energy by day's end.

On the third day in Missouri, Shace leads the group as they reach the northernmost portion of the removal trail in Rolla. Then they head southwest.

There are not many historic stops related to the Trail of Tears in Missouri because at this point during the removal, Cherokee people struggled to survive. Even Reverend Butrick barely wrote in his journal in Missouri, as both he and his wife fought continued illness. Research groups in Missouri today study removal camp and burial sites.

On their journey across the state, the team stops and rests at the same water stops their ancestors used nearly two hundred years before. Community groups support the team. The team enjoys lunch and dinner stops along the way, hosted by local people. Meeting with these groups makes up for the lack of historic sites. They share information about the team's ancestors' experiences in Missouri during the forced removal. And because Missouri is so challenging to cross, the team and support staff have their second (and final) rest day after five days on the road.

Everyone cheers with relief when the riders cross the state line into Arkansas two days later. The team and staff know they are close to home and could be there in three hours by car. But there are still a few places to see in northwest Arkansas, where their ancestors camped before reaching Indian Territory, currently known as Oklahoma.

Kaylee Smith celebrates crossing into Arkansas from Missouri after more than a week of riding through the state.

The first stop is the Pea Ridge National Military Park. Although it is famous as a pivotal United States Civil War battlefield, several detachments of Cherokee people stayed here before that war occurred.

The park superintendent, Kevin Eads, welcomes the group as they enter the visitor center. Then Quapaw Nation Tribal Chairman Joseph Byrd also extends a welcome on behalf of his tribe, whose traditional lands the riders are now on. The United States removed the Quapaw from this area in 1834 across the border into the northeast corner of Indian Territory. The Cherokee Nation's Principal Chief Chuck Hoskin Jr. also meets the riders at the park. He accepts Chairman Byrd's welcome and talks about the history of the dispossession (removal) of Native peoples from their homelands. He shares that it is important to know about other Native Nations' removals because many tribes suffered this fate from the US government. He tells the riders that they spread hope and inspiration by making this trip to honor their ancestors. Chief Hoskin presents an RTR blanket to Quapaw Chairman Byrd, acknowledging their tribes' ongoing intertribal relationship.

The riders then watch a video about the Battle of Pea Ridge, an important battle that secured Arkansas and Missouri for the Union

Cherokee Nation Principal Chief Chuck Hoskin Jr. and CN Education Programs Director Corey Bunch present a RTR blanket to Quapaw Nation Chairman Joseph T. Byrd at Pea Ridge National Military Park. The park lies within the Quapaw Nation's ancestral homelands.

during the Civil War. The heat and humidity build as the group tours the park, learning where Cherokee detachments camped in Ruddick Field and Cox Field. Many Cherokee who passed through this area later fought there during the war.

After leaving Pea Ridge, the group heads south to Springdale. That evening, Kevin Eads and his wife, LaDena, a middle-school principal, host a barbecue dinner for the riders and support staff at her school, where the group plays cornhole, shoots hoops, and unwinds.

The next morning, the steamy air creates fog along the trail. Everyone focuses on filling up their tires and hitting the road, because only about 88 miles remain until they complete the journey!

The various Cherokee detachments did not know where their trail would end. Different groups ended up in Spavinaw, Westville, Stilwell, and other places along the eastern side of the new reservation. None of it was familiar to anyone. But these riders take comfort knowing where their journey ends and that loved ones wait for them.

As the fog lifts, Ronnie leads the group onto a bike trail at Lake Fayetteville that ends on the University of Arkansas's flagship campus in Fayetteville. There the team stops to view a trail monument and sign erected at the edge of campus. The Cherokee Nation marshal coordinates with the local police to get the group an escort through the busy college city. The temperature keeps rising, so riders must continue moving since they have a few spots still to visit on their 50-mile ride today.

Once they reach the Oklahoma state line, everyone stops to take pictures with big smiles. They are getting closer to the Cherokee Nation capital in Tahlequah! The riders head into Westville, where police escort them into town. The fire department's trucks park near the road and . . . *WHOOSH*!

Laughs, smiles, and shrieks erupt from the group as cold, refreshing water hits them from the fire truck's hose. They enjoy an early lunch provided by community members and give interviews to a local newspaper reporter.

From there the group cycles out to Cherokee Nation Industries, a manufacturing company in Stilwell, Oklahoma, owned by the tribe. Fifty employees cheer their arrival and have snacks and cold water waiting.

It's not even one thirty in the afternoon yet, and it's already 91 degrees and feels like it's over 100 with the heat index. What a hot mid-June day! But the Cherokee Nation riders are happy to see familiar faces and places despite the temperature.

After snacks, the cyclists head on to what was known as Mrs. Webber's Plantation during the time of removal. Now it is the Stilwell City Cemetery. More than 3,500 Cherokee people completed their forced removal here.

Since there were no homes waiting for the Cherokee people upon arrival, many camped on the plantation land, which had been arranged by the federal government. Dependent on the food supplied

2021 team under the National Park Service marker within the Cherokee Nation reservation in Stilwell, Oklahoma, showing where some Cherokee people ended their removal journey.

by the US government after entering their new reservation, many Cherokee struggled to stay healthy during the winter and through the spring. Many survivors were injured or ill because of their months-long journey. More died before they could heal.

Even after such a difficult and demoralizing trip, no one could spend time grieving their losses. They needed to work on building homes and planting crops to secure shelter and food. The suffering of the Cherokee Nation lasted long after the arrival to Indian Territory. Removal caused many orphan children. Who would care for them now? Many adults needed care themselves, and everyone needed to get busy rebuilding their lives in a completely foreign place. Visiting the cemetery and understanding its history gives everyone on this year's RTR ride a new perspective about the end of the trail for many Cherokee people.

From the cemetery, the riders cycle on two-lane back roads to Rocky Mountain School. It's located in the Cherokee-speaking community of Rocky Mountain. The late Cherokee Chief Wilma Mankiller and her family are from there.

About a mile before arriving at the school, Whitney, Shace, and Kaylee bump into one another as they head down a hill. Fortunately there are only minor injuries in this fairly big crash. The group made it almost the entire trip without a major collision!

But there's damage to Whitney's bike. It got tangled up when she landed in a ditch. Will must leave the group and take Whitney's bike to get it fixed. Otherwise she will not be able to finish the ride tomorrow. Will drives thirty minutes to the bike shop in Tahlequah, arriving with just enough time to get Whitney's bike repaired before closing.

Back at Rocky Mountain School, some of the riders' families arrive to visit and have dinner with the team. The group spends their final night together here, sleeping on cots in classrooms.

The 2021 team exchanges high fives after reaching the state line near Westville, Oklahoma.

ᎠᏍᏙᏛᎢ 8

ᎠᏂᎷᎬᎢ ᏧᏁᏅᏒ ᎠᎴ ᎦᏙᎤᏍᏗ ᏔᎵᏁ ᏏᏍᎢ

CHAPTER 8

Returning Home and What Comes Next

The next morning the group circles up for one last time to pray and do their war cry. Excitement, sadness, and nervous energy are palpable. Every day for more than three weeks, they have been together: constant companions, confiding joys and sorrows, helping each other stretch to overcome sore muscles, encouraging and comforting one another. What will life be like now? As Tracie leads the team away from Rocky Mountain School, they try to envision how completing this ride has changed them. They pedal up and down curvy back roads toward the Cherokee capital of Tahlequah, about 25 miles.

Before the team finishes the ride, they make a stop at the Illinois River. There a Cherokee medicine person greets them and conducts a private ceremony. This special ceremony's purpose is to bless and comfort the riders after their grueling and emotional ride. It is also meant to remove any possible negative energy brought home by the riders.

As the team approaches Tahlequah, more Cherokee marshals arrive to escort them downtown. The short ride to the return ceremony is live streamed on social media for everyone to see. Prior to this, the team was seen only in social media posts by their tribes, the *Cherokee Phoenix* newspaper, or local media along the route.

Family, friends, and community members gather at the outdoor Cherokee Nation Peace Pavilion for the return ceremony. People line the final few blocks and hold posters that say things like "Welcome home!" "Lookin' good!" and "Proud of you" in English and Cherokee. Some wave the CN and EBCI tribal flags.

The group stops two blocks short of the Peace Pavilion. Each rider takes the time to pin a large flag from their tribe across their back. They also need to wait, because tribal officials aren't yet present to give the riders their medallions and plaques in honor of completing the ride. The tribal leaders are elsewhere in town for the annual tri-council meeting, when the Cherokee Nation, Eastern Band of Cherokee Indians, and United Keetoowah Band all come together. They discuss mutually important issues they want to work on together, such as increasing the number of Cherokee language speakers and preserving cultural sites like Kituwah and others in the homelands.

Thankfully the three chiefs arrive in less than thirty minutes. Now the celebration can start! Laughter, tears, and shouts fill the air. Television and newspaper reporters jockey to interview riders in between hugs from loved ones and eager reunions.

Once the ceremony begins, Crosslin Smith, a Cherokee spiritual leader, offers a prayer. The Cherokee National Youth Choir performs, singing in the Cherokee language. Both the Cherokee Nation and Eastern Band chiefs address the crowd and welcome the riders home. Will asks Kaylee Smith to speak for the Cherokee Nation team, and EBCI selects Raylen Bark to speak about her experiences.

Kaylee Smith sheds tears as she hugs teammate Whitney Roach after arriving home in June 2021.

Kaylee shares, "This was just a small glimpse of what our ancestors endured so long ago. I have learned so many things about being a Cherokee woman and all the responsibilities that come with it. From the beginning, I knew I wanted to educate others about the horrors that happened to our Cherokee ancestors. Many people believe we left by choice—but in reality, our ancestors were driven from our homes. They were beaten, they were raped, and they were forced to live in harsh weather conditions. I didn't feel like I had a purpose in life [before the ride], and I didn't know if I was going to be able to make it. But being with my teammates made me realize I do have a purpose, and I am important. I am a strong Cherokee woman, and I can do anything that I set my mind to."

After Kaylee's powerful presentation, Raylen reveals, "It was really rough and rigorous, as we had to wait two years to complete the ride [due to COVID-19]. But being with my riders from the Eastern Band and others from the Cherokee Nation . . . genuinely completed me."

After their remarks, all nine riders receive their completion medals from their respective chief. Not only do they get to keep their bike, but each cyclist also now joins a select group—Remember the Removal alumni.

2021 Remember the Removal team members pose for a photo after receiving their completion medals and being honored by their tribes.

These cyclists didn't always know how they would get through each part of the ride. As they move forward in life, they will be unsure at times, and having ridden the trail to remember their ancestors' suffering provides them with proof that they can face any hardships that lie ahead. They also better understand the importance of

COMING TOGETHER

Newly medaled RTR alumna Melanie Taylor Giang summed up the experience. "I feel like it's been a huge representation of how Cherokee people across the three different Cherokee tribes are all one people. We can come together to support each other. That's one thing that I've gotten out of this ride," she explained. "Something else I could say would be determination. Over the past two years, the people that are here today have had to be determined in order to stick with this program. I think that's a reflection of our ancestors who were determined to make it through the trail to the final destination point. They didn't know where they were going to be. Likewise we didn't completely know what we were going to go through on this ride."

protecting the health, sovereignty, language, land, and culture of Cherokee people for future generations.

Youth who step up to bravely take on the challenge of riding a bicycle nearly 1,000 miles not only gain leadership skills but become engaged citizens within the Cherokee Nation as they share what they gained and learned with their families and their communities. This is exactly what the ride's creators envisioned when they worked to set up the program many decades ago.

National Park Service signs mark the Trail of Tears through the seven states the RTR team crosses from Georgia to Oklahoma.

EPILOGUE

The Remember the Removal ride continues. Each year, both the Cherokee Nation and the Eastern Band of Cherokee Indians train and support teams that honor their ancestors and the experiences of Cherokee people during the forced removal. Then they jointly celebrate the riders at the end of the journey in Tahlequah each June.

The 2020–2021 riders' lives carry on too. The Cherokee Nation's youngest rider, Shace Duncan, graduated from Sequoyah High School in Tahlequah the year after the ride. He studies environmental biology and Native American studies at Stanford University.

Both Whitney Roach and Kaylee Smith earned their bachelor's degrees from Northeastern State University (NSU). Hearing about Kaylee's experience inspired her brother Jaxen to complete the ride in 2024.

Mel Taylor moved her family to Tahlequah and received her bachelor's degree from NSU. Just before graduating in May 2023, she joined Cherokee Nation Businesses as a culture and tourism coordinator.

Tracie Asbill continues to work as a pediatric nurse practitioner within the Cherokee Nation's healthcare system. Fellow mentor rider Ronnie Duncan still encourages each year's riders when the weather forces them indoors for workouts at the tribe's Markoma Gym.

Will Chavez served as the RTR ride coordinator and team trainer from 2019–2024 and then as the team trainer for the 2025 ride. He still works as the *Cherokee Phoenix*'s assistant editor.

The Eastern Band team's lives kept moving forward too. Both Raylen Bark and Drew Johnson completed their college degrees. Bear Allison continued his photography business and released a film about Cherokee basket makers, titled *Weaving Connections*, in 2022. Corlee Thomas-Hill served as coordinator and trainer for the EBCI teams through the 2022 ride.

On July 8, 2024, the nonprofit organization called Remember the Removal Legacy Association, made up of RTR alumni, hosted a fortieth-anniversary gala. With support from the Cherokee Nation and others, the event honored the inaugural riders. Many 1984 team members attended and shared how their experiences during their nearly month-long ride shaped their lives. There were lots of teary faces in the crowd after listening to their powerful stories!

The annual Remember the Removal ride continues to connect today's Cherokee people with their ancestors, history, culture, and language. It also creates a strong desire to serve others. Most important, the alumni and each year's new group of riders educate others about the tremendous harm the US government caused Cherokee people through the removal, and how it has lasted long after the forced march. Those who participate go on to serve others with their gifts and abilities, which is a core part of their Cherokee values, and just as the ride's two creators intended over four decades ago.

Remember the Removal alumni include doctors, attorneys, coaches, teachers, journalists, nurses, and other professionals. For example, Joseph Erb, 2014 and 2015 ride coordinator, worked with other Cherokee people to help tech companies such as Google, Apple, and Microsoft incorporate the Cherokee language into their platforms and software. Dr. Amber Anderson Buettner, a 2016 RTR alumna, works as a research epidemiologist at the University of Oklahoma's College of Public Health doing research on health disparities among

American Indians. And Raven Girty, a 2017 RTR alumna, works for Williams Companies in Tulsa as a supply-chain governance and strategy business analyst. She reflected on the ride, "I pushed myself past my own mental and physical barriers, which taught me that I am so much stronger than I think that I am."

What a powerful legacy for this program, especially given its humble roots!

The original 1984 team with 19 riders reaches the Oklahoma state line.

1785—Treaty of Hopewell is the first treaty signed by the Cherokee with the new United States after the Revolutionary War with Great Britain. Signed on November 28 on the Hopewell Plantation in South Carolina, the treaty cedes much of the lands along the French Broad and Holston Rivers.

1789—US Constitution ratified. Federal government redesigned, granting US Congress exclusive authority to regulate commerce with Native Nations.

1791—Treaty of Holston signed on July 7, establishing relationship terms with the United States and placing Cherokee towns under protection of the United States.

1817—Treaty of Cherokee Agency signed on July 8, providing benefits for Cherokees who choose to move west and also benefitting those who choose to stay.

1819—With the Calhoun Treaty signed on February 27, the United States purchases land near the Hiwassee, Little Tennessee, and Big Tennessee Rivers in Tennessee. After this land cessation, the Cherokee National Council declares the tribe will cede no more land.

1821—Sequoyah (also known by his English name, George Guess or George Gist) completes his creation of a written version of the Cherokee language. Unlike English, which uses letters to form syllables and then combines them to form words, the Cherokee language does not have letters and uses symbols that represent syllables to make words. Sequoyah invents a symbol for each syllable so Cherokee people can write in their language. After the Cherokee Nation officially adopts the syllabary, more than 90 percent of its citizens can read the language within months.

1828—The *Cherokee Phoenix* prints its first edition in Cherokee and English on February 21 in New Echota, the Cherokee Nation's capital (in what is now northern Georgia). The newspaper is a critical information source, helping Cherokee citizens stay involved in the ongoing fight against removal.

1830—Georgia enacts a land lottery using Cherokee lands. Thousands of Georgians flood onto Cherokee lands, which increases the suffering for Cherokee people.

1832—The Cherokee Nation turns to the US Supreme Court to protect its rights. The court rules in favor of Cherokee sovereignty in *Worcester v. Georgia*. However, Georgia, with the support of President Andrew Jackson, refuses to honor the ruling.

1835—Twenty Cherokee citizens, part of a small group in favor of removal (known as the Treaty Party), sign the Treaty of New Echota on December 29 with US government officials. The Treaty Party's leadership claims to represent 16,000 citizens of the Cherokee Nation, but none of the men has authority from the Principal Chief and the Cherokee National Council to sign. The treaty states that the tribe will give up its remaining lands in the east for $5 million. The Cherokee have two years from the date of the treaty's ratification to prepare and move. The treaty is ratified by the US Senate on May 23, 1836.

1838—The voluntary removal deadline of May 23 passes with only 2,000 Cherokees having moved west. US soldiers and state militia begin rounding up Cherokees in Alabama, Tennessee, North Carolina, and Georgia. Nearly 10,000 Cherokees are driven into various internment camps near Fort Cass, by present-day Charleston, Tennessee.

1838—After three detachments of Cherokee are sent west by boat on the Tennessee River in June, the government is forced to stop transporting people this way because a drought lowers the water level. The remaining Cherokee are forced to camp around southeastern Tennessee and northeastern Alabama to await removal during what turns out to be one of the hottest summers on record for the area.

1838—Cherokee who remain in the internment camps during the summer are plagued by malaria, dysentery, cholera, and other diseases. It's estimated that approximately 1,500 Cherokee die in the camps while waiting to be moved west.

1838—Cherokee leaders request to delay the removal of remaining Cherokees until the fall, which is granted. General Winfield Scott also grants the Cherokee permission to manage their own removal with expenses deducted from the money paid to the tribe by the federal government for the Cherokee Nation's land.

1838—The first detachment departs Tennessee for Indian Territory in August, led by Hair Conrad. Approximately 700 people are in the detachment. During their five-month journey, there are 9 births, 57 deaths, and 24 transfers, leaving 654 people who arrive west on January 17, 1839. Some who were too sick to continue "transferred" or joined a later detachment that came through in order to continue the trip when they were healthier.

1838—Thirteen detachments, organized by Chief Ross and led by Cherokee men, begin moving west in October. They take three to five months to reach Indian Territory, an 800-mile journey. A harsh winter, frozen rivers, and other difficulties prolong the travel time of some detachments. It's estimated that approximately 4,000 Cherokee die from sickness, exposure, and injuries during the roundup, in internment camps, while traveling on the trail, and after reaching Indian Territory.

About 660 members of the Treaty Party and those who are supportive of removal leave Calhoun, Tennessee, and head due west across the state toward Memphis and then through Arkansas. This detachment has a US military escort and is not organized by Chief Ross and other Cherokee leaders. Their route takes only 89 days, and they have better weather than most Cherokee experience on the Northern Route. They still lose 23 lives on the journey. Those under Chief Ross's direction did not travel this route because of the lack of adequate camping places and provisions in the swampy Arkansas landscapes for much larger groups.

1839—The Taylor detachment, the final one to arrive, gets to Indian Territory on March 23.

1839—Those Cherokee who voluntarily relocated in the 1780s to northeastern Arkansas, other Cherokee who moved themselves before the internment camps, the Treaty Party members, and those forcibly removed all come together to sign a new constitution to govern the Cherokee Nation on September 6.

REMEMBER THE REMOVAL RIDE HISTORY

1984—First Remember the Removal ride

1985–2008—Hiatus

2009—Remember the Removal ride becomes an annual event for the Cherokee Nation.

2011—Eastern Band of Cherokee Indians joins the Cherokee Nation for the annual ride.

2017—The Cherokee Nation opens the RTR ride up to those aged 35 or older to apply as mentor riders. 1984 RTR alumnus Will Chavez is the first selected mentor rider. While nothing in the contract states that anyone *has* to mentor the younger riders, they are told to set a good example and be supportive. There is not always a mentor rider for the annual ride.

2019—Riders are selected for the 2020 ride.

2020—Cherokee Nation cancels the ride due to the COVID-19 pandemic to ensure everyone's safety.

2021—Six Cherokee Nation citizens (four younger riders and two mentor riders) receive their COVID-19 vaccinations and pass the physical exam and the 60-mile road test to participate in the ride. They are joined by three riders from the Eastern Band of Cherokee Indians.

2022—Remember the Removal has its first all-woman group of riders from the Cherokee Nation. The 2023 team ends up being all women as well.

2024—The Remember the Removal fortieth-anniversary gala honors the 1984 inaugural riders.

REMEMBER THE REMOVAL RIDE ANNUAL TIMELINE

August—Applications are available for Cherokee Nation citizens aged 16 to 24, as well as for those aged 35 or older who want to be mentor riders.

September—Applications are due. Interviews are held and selections made for youth and mentor riders.

December—Riders begin history, language, and culture courses as well as physical training sessions each weekend. They ride training bikes outside or work out together in the gym. Each team member also exercises on their own during the week. The Cherokee Nation delivers a road bicycle for each rider.

January–May—The team continues their history, culture, and language courses along with physical training. The team rides outside when weather permits.

May—Each rider must pass a physical exam and complete an untimed 60-mile ride. The Cherokee Nation hosts a send-off ceremony in its capital, Tahlequah, Oklahoma, for everyone to gather before the team heads east for its ride.

Mid-June—The Cherokee Nation hosts a welcome-home ceremony for all riders (both from Cherokee Nation and Eastern Band of Cherokee Indians) to celebrate and reunite with family and friends. Each rider receives a medallion, keeps their bike, and becomes part of the Remember the Removal alumni.

Riding the Trail coauthors Traci Sorell and Will Chavez.

ᏩᏙ (wah-DOE) Thank You!

This book would not have been possible without the 2020–2021 Remember the Removal (RTR) riders; all ride alumni; the support of the Cherokee Nation (administration, tribal council, education services, marshal service, communications, emergency medical services, finance, government relations, health services, and geographic information system services); all ride support staff; Wyman Kirk, who taught the history, language, and culture course and shared his research; the *Cherokee Phoenix*; the Eastern Band of Cherokee Indians; the National Trail of Tears Association chapters in North Carolina, Georgia, Tennessee, Kentucky, Illinois, Missouri, Arkansas, and Oklahoma; and the Remember the Removal Advisory Committee. Wado for all of your help and support! Special wados to Principal Chief Chuck Hoskin Jr. for permitting Traci to follow the 2021 ride; to CN Communications, Tom Fields, Lisa Roach, and Will for use of their photos; to National Trail of Tears Association President Jack Baker for reviewing the text, and to John Ross, first language Cherokee speaker and freelance translator, who crafted the chapter titles in the Cherokee syllabary; and to Cherokee artist Mary Lupton, who created the maps on pages x and 12.

In addition, deep gratitude extends to the entire bookmaking team at Charlesbridge, particularly Senior Editor Karen Boss and Creative Director Diane Earley, and also to our literary agent, Emily Mitchell.

PROCEEDS

Both authors will donate all net proceeds from this book to the Remember the Removal Legacy Association, which supports the ride's alumni in their continuing efforts to educate the public about the Cherokee Nation's forced removal. To learn more about this special organization, visit **www.rtrla.org.**

The Remember the Removal Legacy Association (RTRLA) is a nonprofit educational organization made up of those who have completed the RTR ride. The logo was created by 2012 ride alumna Nathalie Standingcloud.

FROM TRACI SORELL

This book would not have been possible without the financial support and encouragement provided by the Tulsa Artist Fellowship in 2021 and 2022. I also thank my family and friends for their unwavering support and continuous prayers, which helped me complete this work.

I am especially grateful my ancestors survived the internment camps and forced removal to help rebuild the Cherokee Nation, making it possible for me to share this story now. That also would not have been possible without Will Chavez's commitment to the RTR ride and his dedication to educating people about the forced removal and mentoring our Cherokee youth for so many years. I appreciate his longtime service as an editor, reporter, and photographer for the *Cherokee Phoenix*, which shines a spotlight on Cherokee people, their contributions, our language, and our culture.

Understanding what my ancestors and other Cherokee and Freedmen people collectively experienced during the forced removal has changed my life forever. That this book had its genesis just before the COVID-19 pandemic made it all the more difficult to write and complete. The continued losses I experienced among my loved ones as well as those who died across the Cherokee Nation and the world hit hard. I encourage future generations to turn away from colonizing behaviors like land dispossession, violence, internment, and forced removals to protect all living beings on this planet.

FROM WILL CHAVEZ

I would like to thank the many brave and courageous people who have taken the journey to honor and remember their Cherokee ancestors through the Remember the Removal bicycle ride. All of us better understand, especially after completing the ride, how much our ancestors sacrificed and fought for us to be here today. We are proud to come from such resilient people.

Three of my children and numerous cousins have made the 950-mile journey across seven states to bring attention to this horrible time in Cherokee and American history. Our motto for the ride is "Never Forget." We will *never* forget!

Many thank-yous to author Traci Sorell for asking me to help with this story. I am thankful for her continued efforts to capture and share our Cherokee history, culture, and language. It is needed after the loss of so much due in part to the forced removals.

Lastly I must thank my mother, Reba Rodgers, for her encouragement and for buying me my first ten-speed so I could train for the first Remember the Removal ride in 1984. I dedicated that first ride to my late grandfather, William Pettit, who passed in 1982. He and my grandmother Cynthia were the foundation for my continued appreciation of my Cherokeeness. I miss them immensely.

SOURCE NOTES

Epigraph, p. vi: "Let us . . . voice of the people": The Trail of Tears Association, Oklahoma Chapter. *Cherokee Removal: The Journal of Rev. Daniel S. Butrick, May 19, 1838–April 1, 1839*. Park Hill, OK: Trail of Tears Association, 1998, p. 23.

Chapter 1, page 5: "I have no . . . to the West": Jackson, Andrew, "To the Cherokee Tribe of Indians East of the Mississippi River." Digital Public Library of America. https://dp.la/item/485ede64f61268ebc5febe30be9900a6.

Chapter 2, pages 8–9: "wanted . . . culture," "looked forward . . . my home," "There were . . . were kings!": Will Chavez interview with Taylor Alsenay, July 29, 2022.

Chapter 2, page 10: "Oh . . . gone," "I thought . . . disappeared": Traci Sorell discussion with Will Chavez, July 2022.

Chapter 2, sidebar, page 10: "I'm on a . . . quit," "I know . . . times": Will Chavez interview with Marvin Cochran, June 23, 2015.

Chapter 2, page 11: "This is . . . camps": Will Chavez interview with Taylor Alsenay, July 29, 2022.

Chapter 2, page 13: "Bear in mind . . . State Park": Will Chavez interview with Taylor Alsenay, July 29, 2022.

Chapter 3, sidebar, page 23: "Training was hard . . . into this ride": Chavez, Will. "'Remember the Removal' Cyclists Find Strength, Develop Leadership Skills." *Cherokee Phoenix*, June 20, 2018. www.cherokeephoenix.org/culture/remember-the-removal-cyclists-find-strength-develop-leadership-skills/article_99240f32-2899-5dc0-a5c0-44cfd158e55f.html.

Chapter 3, page 26: "I'm usually . . . little shell": Will Chavez interview with Hadyn Jackson, June 11, 2013.

Chapter 5, page 44: "I'm a human . . . happened here": Presentation by Melissa Woody, Hiwassee River Heritage Center, June 1, 2021.

Chapter 5, page 45: "the struggle . . . personal level": Hiwassee River Heritage Center. "The Footsteps." www.hiwasseeheritage.com/the-footsteps.

Chapter 5, page 46: "It's becoming . . . [the ancestors]": Traci Sorell interview with Shace Duncan, June 1, 2021.

Chapter 5, page 49: flatboats: National Park Service, Trail of Tears National Historic Site "Flatboats: Transportation During the Cherokee Removal, 1837–1839." www.nps.gov/articles/000/flatboats-transportation-during-the-cherokee-removal-1837-1839.htm.

Chapter 5, page 49: "After this point . . . from here": Will Chavez's comments at Blythe Ferry, June 1, 2021.

Chapter 6, sidebar, page 53: "Monday . . . Warren County, Tenn": The Trail of Tears Association, Oklahoma Chapter. *Cherokee Removal: The Journal of Rev. Daniel S. Butrick, May 19, 1838–April 1, 1839*. Park Hill, OK: Trail of Tears Association, 1998. pp. 43–44.

Chapter 6, page 55: "A couple of . . . stacked children": Traci Sorell interview with Kaylee Smith, June 16, 2021.

Chapter 6, page 58: "A violation . . . the removal": Presentation by David Britton, Port Royal State Park, June 4, 2021.

The Port Royal Experience sidebar, pages 60–61: all quotations: Traci Sorell interview with each rider, June 16, 2021.

Chapter 6, page 63: "If I saw . . . passed through": Traci Sorell interview with Ronnie Duncan, June 16, 2021.

Chapter 7, page 66: white people . . . burying him! The Trail of Tears Association, Oklahoma Chapter. *Cherokee Removal: The Journal of Rev. Daniel S. Butrick, May 19, 1838–April 1, 1839*. Park Hill, OK: Trail of Tears Association, 1998. pp. 49–54, 55.

Chapter 7, sidebar, page 67: "I have been . . . try to help": Will Chavez interview with José Alcalá, June 14, 2023.

Chapter 7, page 70: He accepts . . . intertribal relationship. Presentation by Cherokee Nation Principal Chief Chuck Hoskin Jr., June 16, 2021.

Chapter 8, pages 77–78: "This was just . . . my mind to," "It was really rough . . . completed me": Douglas, Blake. "Cherokee Cyclists Complete 'Remember the Removal' Ride, Reflect on Challenges Ancestors Faced on Trail of Tears." https://keyt.com/cnn-regional/2021/06/20/cherokee-cyclists-complete-remember-the-removal-ride-reflect-on-challenges-ancestors-faced-on-trail-of-tears.

Chapter 8, sidebar, page 79: "I feel like . . . with this ride": Traci Sorell interview with Melanie Taylor Giang, June 16, 2021.

Epilogue, page 83: "I pushed myself . . . think that I am": Chavez, Will. "Girty Enjoying Working for Williams and Continues to Move Up in Company." *Cherokee Phoenix*, March 29, 2024. www.cherokeephoenix.org/people/girty-enjoying-working-for-williams-and-continues-to-move-up-in-company/article_c248a34c-ed3b-11ee-b7ab-47f185fd7db4.html.

SELECTED BIBLIOGRAPHY

Butler, Mrs. Elizur (Lucy). American Board of Commissioners for Foreign Missions Archives, ABC 1-91, Box 13. Houghton Library, Harvard College Library.

Gibson, Wayne Dell. "Cherokee Treaty Party Moves West: The Bell-Deas Overland Journey, 1838–1839." Oklahoma City: The Gateway to Oklahoma History /Oklahoma Historical Society, 2001. https://gateway.okhistory.org/ark:/67531 /metadc2016841.

National Park Service. Trail of Tears: National Historic Trail. www.nps.gov/trte

Perdue, Theda, and Michael D. Green. *The Cherokee Nation and the Trail of Tears.* New York: Viking/Penguin, 2007.

Smith, Samuel D. "Military Sites Archaeology in Tennessee." *Tennessee Historical Quarterly* 59, no. 3 (2000): 140–157. www.tn.gov/content/dam/tn/environment /archaeology/documents/staffpubs/arch_Smith%202000.pdf.

Tennessee River Valley. Cherokee Removal Memorial Park at Historic Blythe Ferry. https://tennesseerivervalleygeotourism.org/entries/cherokee-removal-memorial -park-at-historic-blythe-ferry/d2a64d12-f649-427c-b415-26363b2a0df9.

Asbill, Tracie. "Opinion: Forever Grateful for 'Remember the Removal' Experience." *Cherokee Phoenix*, October 2, 2021. www.cherokeephoenix.org/opinion/opinion-forever-grateful-for-remember-the-removal-experience/article_9b9c7b92-2317-11ec-8b1e-275419a56c39.html.

Chavez, Will. "'Remember the Removal' Founder Shares Story of Ride's Beginning." *Cherokee Phoenix*, May 28, 2024. www.cherokeephoenix.org/people/remember-the-removal-founder-shares-story-of-ride-s-beginning/article_deb99004-1d38-11ef-ae38-87e7a8c602bd.html.

Cherokee Nation. "1984 RTR Bike Ride Full Documentary." www.youtube.com/watch?v=8pR9IQptHvw.

Cherokee Nation. ᎾᏍᎩ ᎠᏅᏓᏗᏍᏗ ᏗᎨᏥᎧᏬᏍᏒᎢ "Remember the Removal Bike Ride 2021 Journey." www.facebook.com/TheCherokeeNation/videos/remember-the-removal-bike-ride-2021-journey/323272409419988.

Cherokee Phoenix. "2021 'Remember the Removal' Cyclists Receive Sendoff." May 28, 2021. www.youtube.com/watch?v=CREb9LbTZwY.

Cherokee Phoenix. "Quapaw Leaders Meet 'Remember the Removal' Cyclists in Arkansas." June 18, 2021. www.youtube.com/watch?v=g4MOA-IPQbI.

Cherokee Phoenix. "'Remember the Removal' Cyclists Return." June 20, 2021. www.youtube.com/watch?v=kMJ_QDn9HaA.

Hill, Nick. "Eternal Flame Returns to Red Clay State Park." WDEF News 12, November 12, 2022. www.wdef.com/eternal-flame-returns-to-red-clay-state-park.

Missouri Humanities. "Si Otsedoha (We Are Still Here): Remembering Cherokee Removal." January 19, 2023. www.youtube.com/watch?v=OdMKxXgCHOI.

Osiyo TV: Voices of the Cherokee People. "Remember the Removal." https://osiyo.tv/?s=remember+the+removal.

Tennessee State Parks. "Dunbar Cave State Park." https://tnstateparks.com/parks/dunbar-cave.

Tennessee State Parks. "Port Royal State Historic Park." https://tnstateparks.com/parks/port-royal.

IMAGE CREDITS

All images used with permission.

Jacket: © Cherokee Nation Communications

Title page: © Cherokee Nation Communications

Pages ii–iii: © Cherokee Nation Communications

Page vii: © Cherokee Nation Communications

Page viii: © Cherokee Nation Communications

Page x: © Mary Lupton

Page xi: © Cherokee Nation Communications

Page xii: Library of Congress Geography and Map Division (LCCN: 99446145)

Page 4: Library of Congress Geography and Map Division (LCCN: 99446197)

Page 6: © Tom Fields

Page 8: Image of letter courtesy of Tress Yahola Lewis

Page 9: Created by Tom Fields

Page 10: © Tom Fields

Page 12: © Mary Lupton

Page 14: © Cherokee Nation Communications

Page 15: © Cherokee Nation Communications

Page 16: © Cherokee Nation Communications (Ronnie Duncan); © Chad Hunter/*Cherokee Phoenix* (Will Chavez)

Page 17: © Cherokee Choices

Page 18: © Will Chavez

Page 20: © Will Chavez/*Cherokee Phoenix*

Page 22: © Will Chavez

Page 23: © Cherokee Nation Communications

Page 24: © Will Chavez/*Cherokee Phoenix*

Page 25: © Lisa Roach

Page 28: © Will Chavez/*Cherokee Phoenix*

Page 30: © Will Chavez/*Cherokee Phoenix*

Page 31: © Will Chavez/*Cherokee Phoenix*

Page 32: © Will Chavez/*Cherokee Phoenix*

Page 34: © Will Chavez/*Cherokee Phoenix*

Page 36: © Cherokee Nation Communications

Page 38: © Cherokee Nation Communications

Page 40: © Cherokee Nation Communications

Page 41: © Cherokee Nation Communications

Page 45: © Will Chavez/*Cherokee Phoenix*

Page 47: © Cherokee Nation Communications

Page 48: © Cherokee Nation Communications

Page 49: © Will Chavez/*Cherokee Phoenix*

Page 50: © Cherokee Nation Communications

Page 52: © Cherokee Nation Communications

Page 55: © Will Chavez/*Cherokee Phoenix*

Page 56: © Cherokee Nation Communications

Page 57: © Cherokee Nation Communications

Page 59: © Will Chavez/*Cherokee Phoenix*

Page 62: © Will Chavez/*Cherokee Phoenix*

Page 63: © Will Chavez/*Cherokee Phoenix*

Page 64: © Will Chavez/*Cherokee Phoenix*

Page 66: © Will Chavez/*Cherokee Phoenix*

Page 67: © Will Chavez/*Cherokee Phoenix*

Page 69: © Will Chavez/*Cherokee Phoenix*

Page 70: © Will Chavez/*Cherokee Phoenix*

Page 72: © Will Chavez/*Cherokee Phoenix*

Page 74: © Cherokee Nation Communications

Page 77: © Cherokee Nation Communications

Page 78: © Cherokee Nation Communications

Page 80: © Will Chavez/*Cherokee Phoenix*

Page 83: © Tom Fields

Page 90: © Chad Hunter/*Cherokee Phoenix*

Page 91: courtesy of the Remember the Removal Legacy Association (RTRLA)

INDEX

Page numbers in *italics* refer to photos and illustrations.

INDEX